To Erica and Ebba—With all my love.

OCEAN BEACH

Douglas Ljungkvist

KEHRER

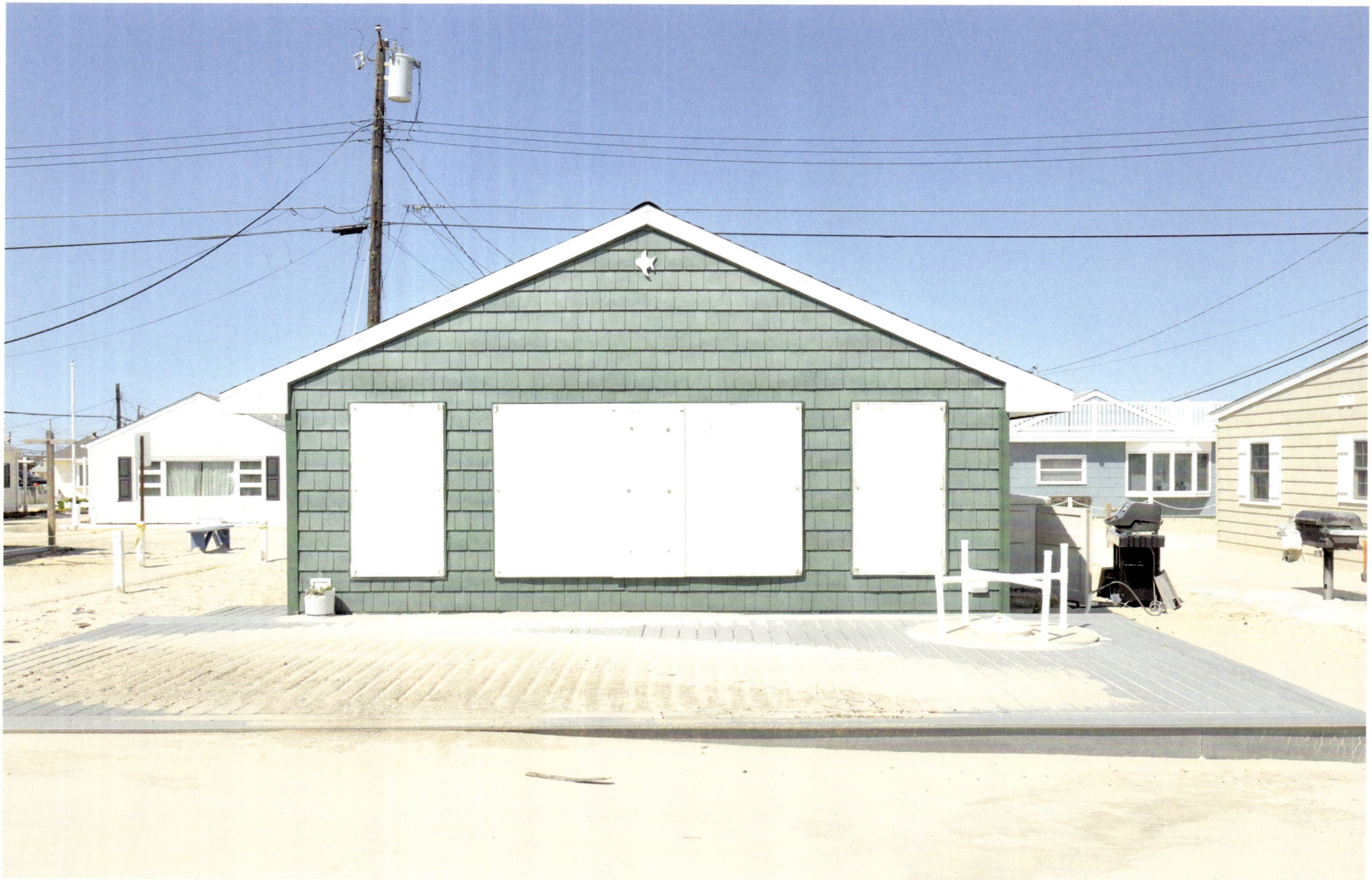

TIME PRESENT—TIME PAST

Harvey Benge

You might ask what could possibly induce camera artist Douglas Ljungkvist to visit, let alone decide to work in, Ocean Beach, this humdrum and mega-ordinary spit of sand that runs for 200 miles along the Atlantic. This is a destination offering little more than rows and rows of bungalows arranged in uninspiring ranks flanking streets made of sand. Spare and spartan, with only the *ubiquitous* Dairy Queen offering relief from such visual monotony. No way is Ocean Beach The Hamptons. North of Good Luck Point, with the compass pointing east, the prospect of the drive along Little League World Champions Boulevard toward the ocean seems to offer little reward or prospects of excitement.——For Ljungkvist, this project is an investigation of change, of the hard fact that nothing lasts forever. It is also about beauty, sad beauty, beauty gilded with impermanence. And time present and time past, a past that informs the future.——At first sight, the pictures appear to be simple documentary photographs made in the vein of what you see is what you get. But wait, there is more. These are not simply straight records, they are loaded and layered, and have a prosaic style that lends the work its strength. There is no getting away from these quietly unforgiving photographs. We are face to face with the anonymous ambiguity of ordinary places, perhaps as a metaphor for the human condition—certainly that in the First World, where to be always bright and cheerful is mandatory at all costs. ——Ljungkvist has produced a critique of banality—a profound political and social statement. These pictures address issues of conformity and of pervasive empty consumerism. We are confronted with a bizarre version of the American Dream that embodies the unrelenting desire for happiness constructed from a determined yet fragile sense of self-value and apple-pie radiant optimism. The photographs speak of the yearning to belong; they consider the very nature of shelter, place and space and how—just like among animals—territory is staked out. Individualism is nonetheless proclaimed despite the grinding ordinariness and depressing sameness.——And yet —there is something peculiar going on in these photographs. What are we actually looking at? On the one hand, there is a sense of the Hollywood backdrop with colored flats propped up with 4 x 2s. Bates Motel is next door—a place of hurried meetings and departures. At the same time, could we not also be looking at some bizarre internment camp? These pictures suggest a sense of apocalyptic abandonment lingering in the damp salty air.——Offered few clues, we are forced to create a narrative out of our own experience. There is a theatrical sense of temporality. Time—past, present and future—seems frozen, museum-like, into dioramas or stage sets. Human presence is intimated rather than revealed in these pictures, and you are left to wonder who might have stayed in these places. We construct identities for the unidentified people who have come and gone looking for happy days. Fun at any price.——Ljungkvist invites us into bedrooms and kitchens and living spaces redolent of the set of a way-off-Broadway production of a walk-on walk-off bedroom farce. We discover insignificant everyday objects that have much to tell, often about the idea of escape—palm-tree motifs, a suitcase, a ship's wheel and the inevitable big-screen TV. Escape from what? ——There are a number of parallels in Ljungkvist's *Ocean Beach* work with Lewis Baltz's *The Tract Houses* series (1969–71). Baltz's unmediated black-and-white photographs depict the graceless efficiencies of the new suburbs that were springing up in California at that time. They are anti-authoritarian documents offering a critique of suburban banality. Ljungkvist's work has opted for the flipside of that formal coin which, despite its pastel prettiness, offers an equally critical view of American suburban culture.——These photographs do not ask us to judge—after all, each of us wants to stake out our own territory, feel safe, find fulfilment, feel happy. Even if these conditions are achievable, permanence is not. Here at Ocean Beach, amid streets made of sand, the inevitability of change seems to strike us wherever we look. The sand speaks of perpetual impermanence and an elusive dream. Were we not once exhorted to build our house on solid rock like a wise man?——Not an option at Ocean Beach. We wait for the inevitable to happen. Tick tock.

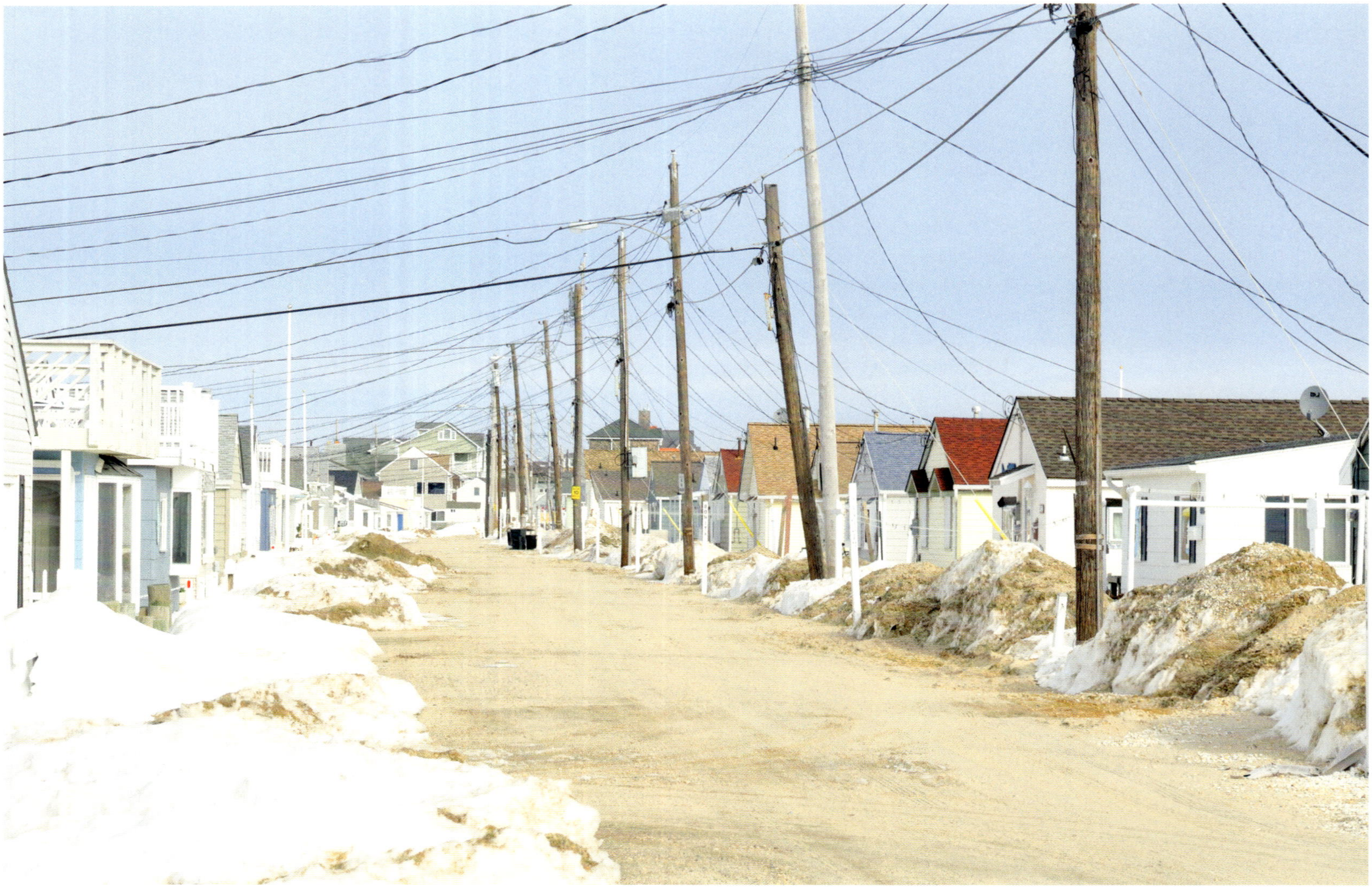

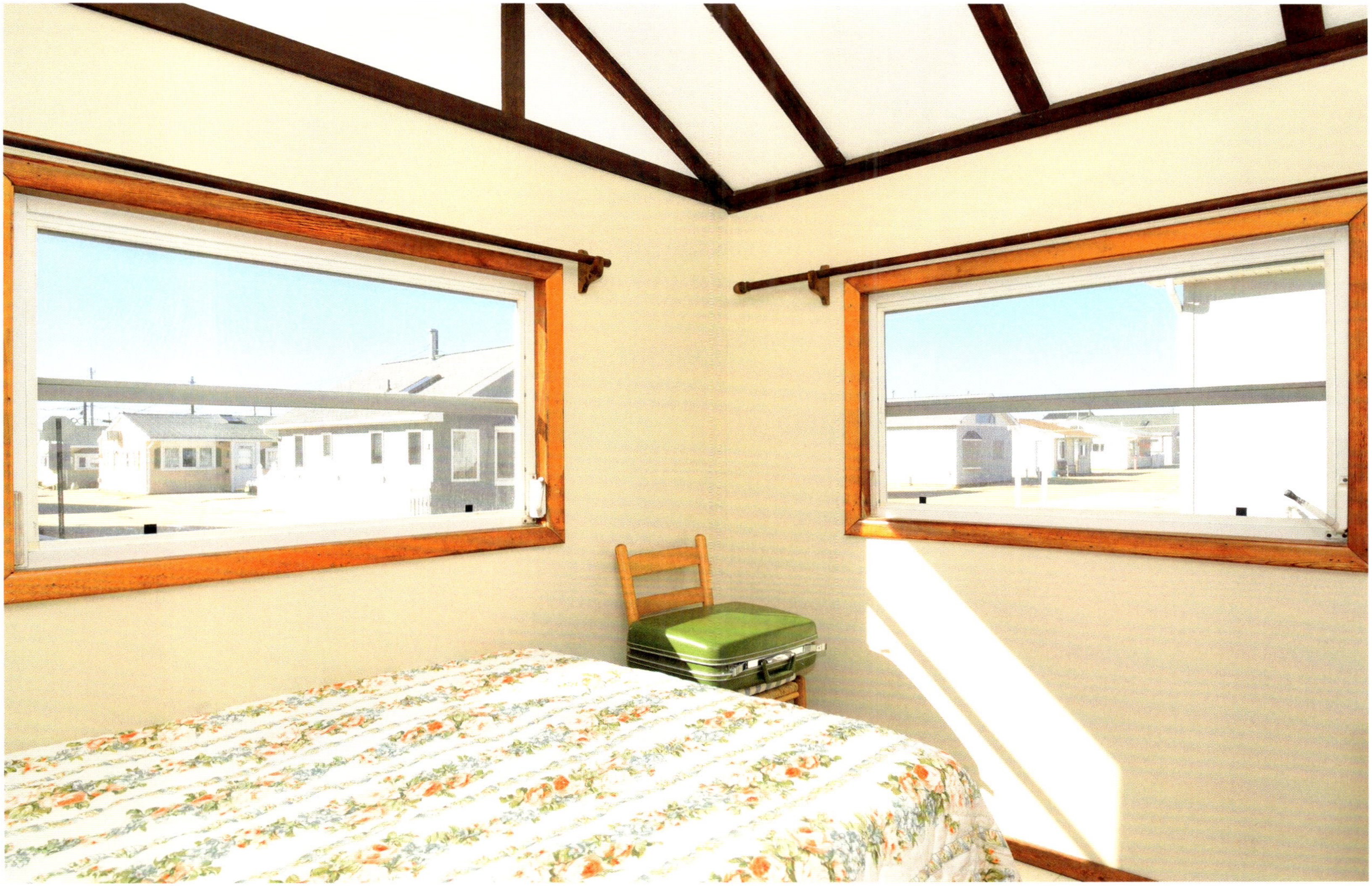

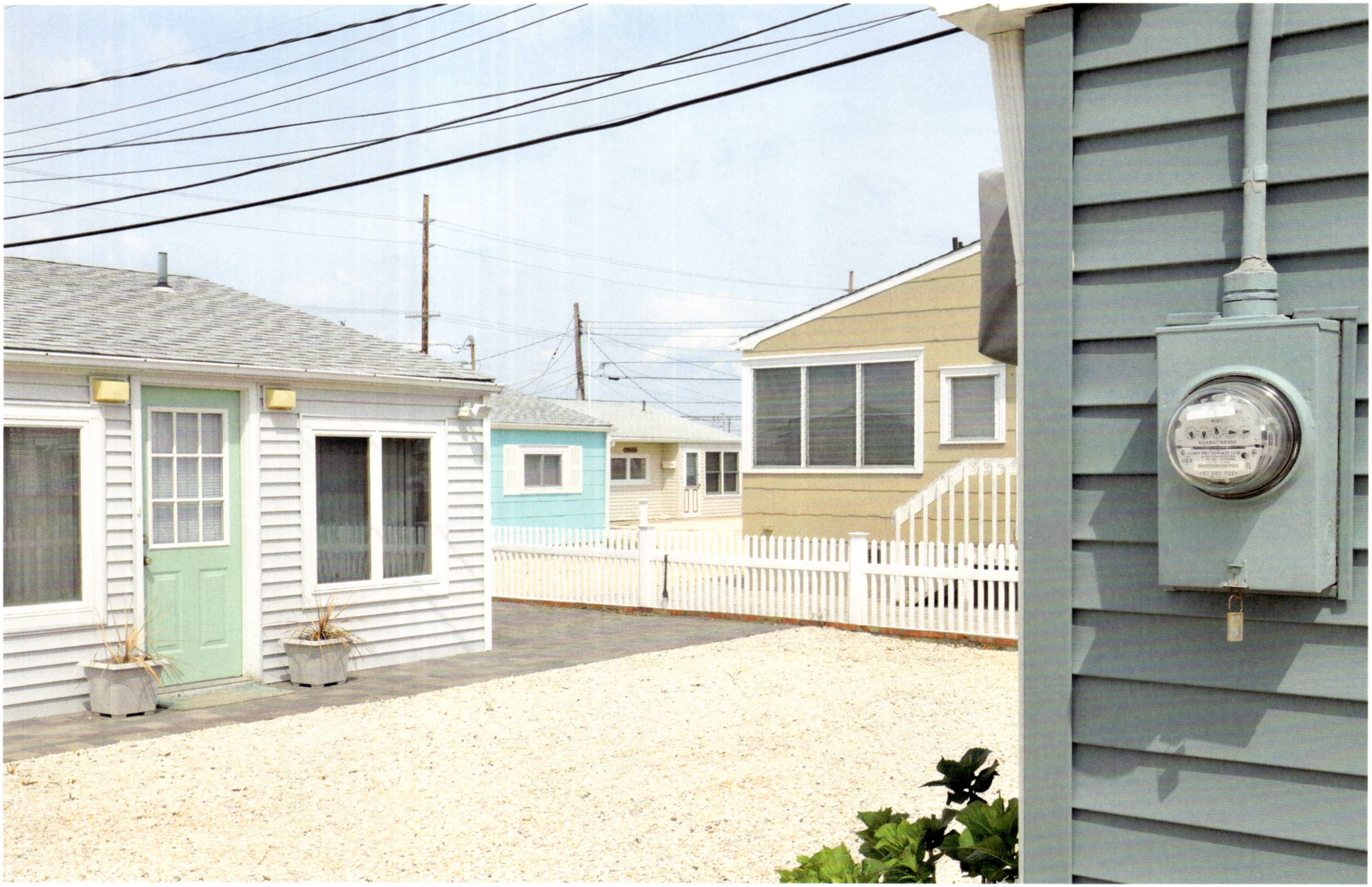

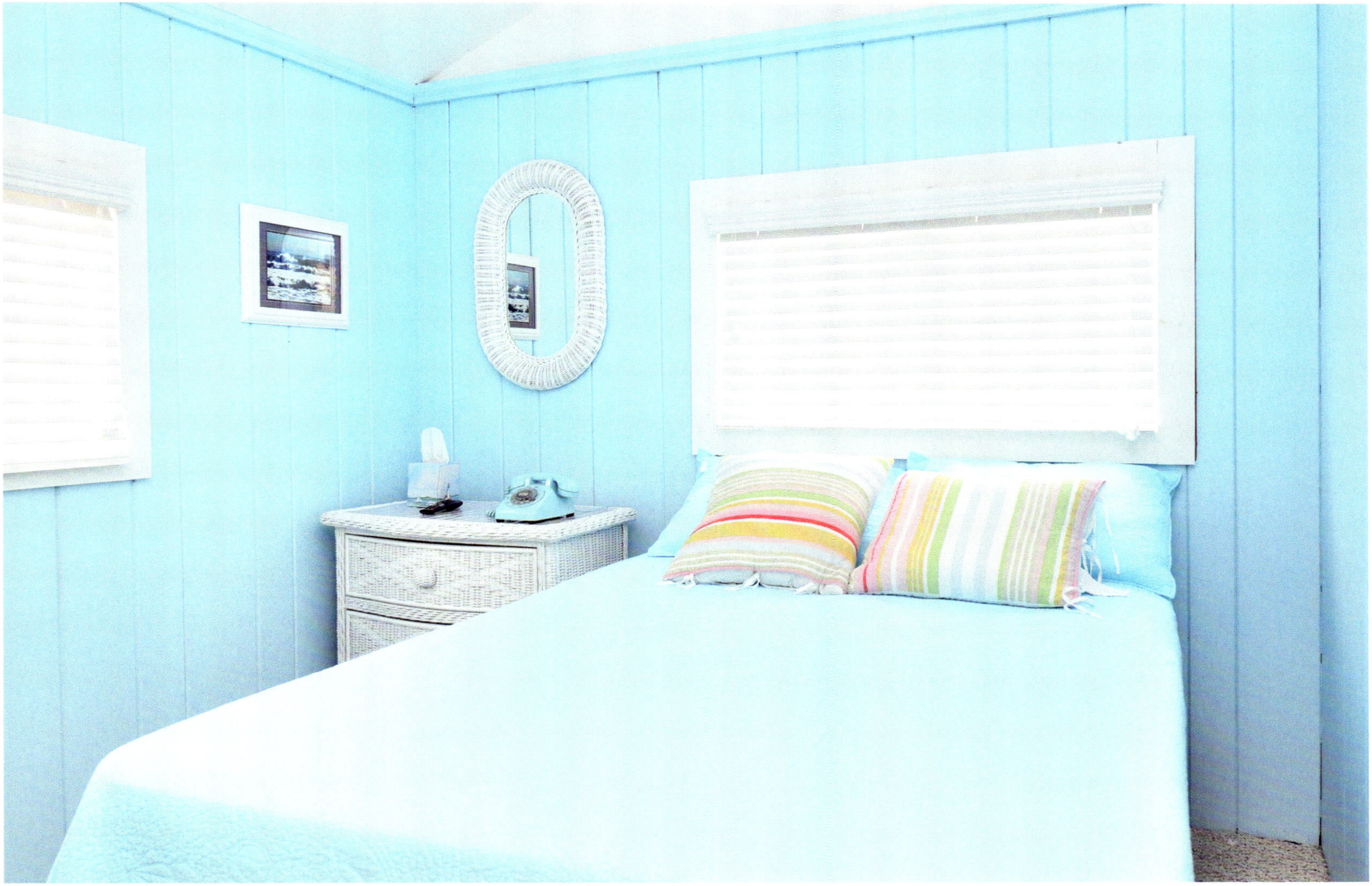

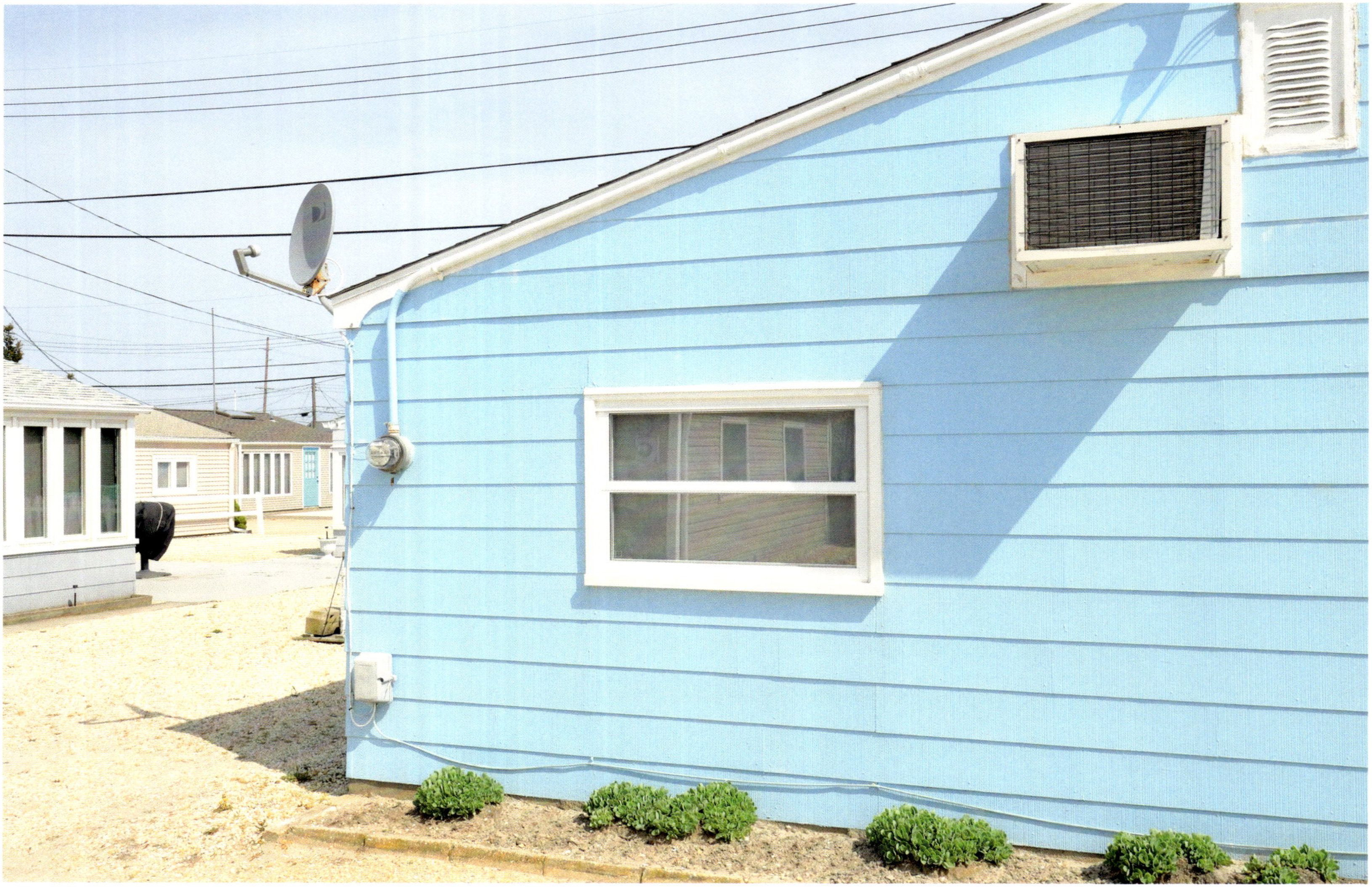

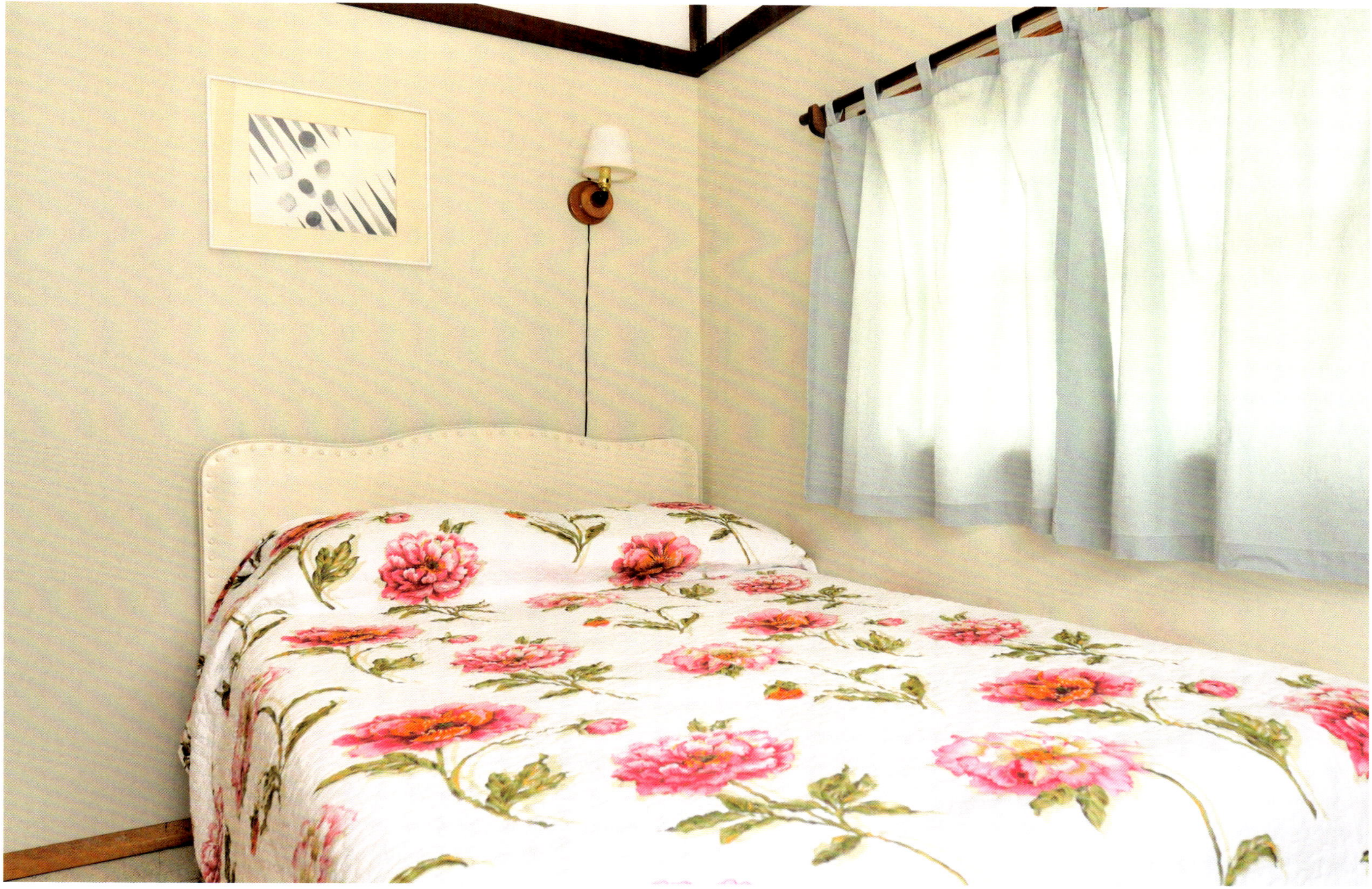

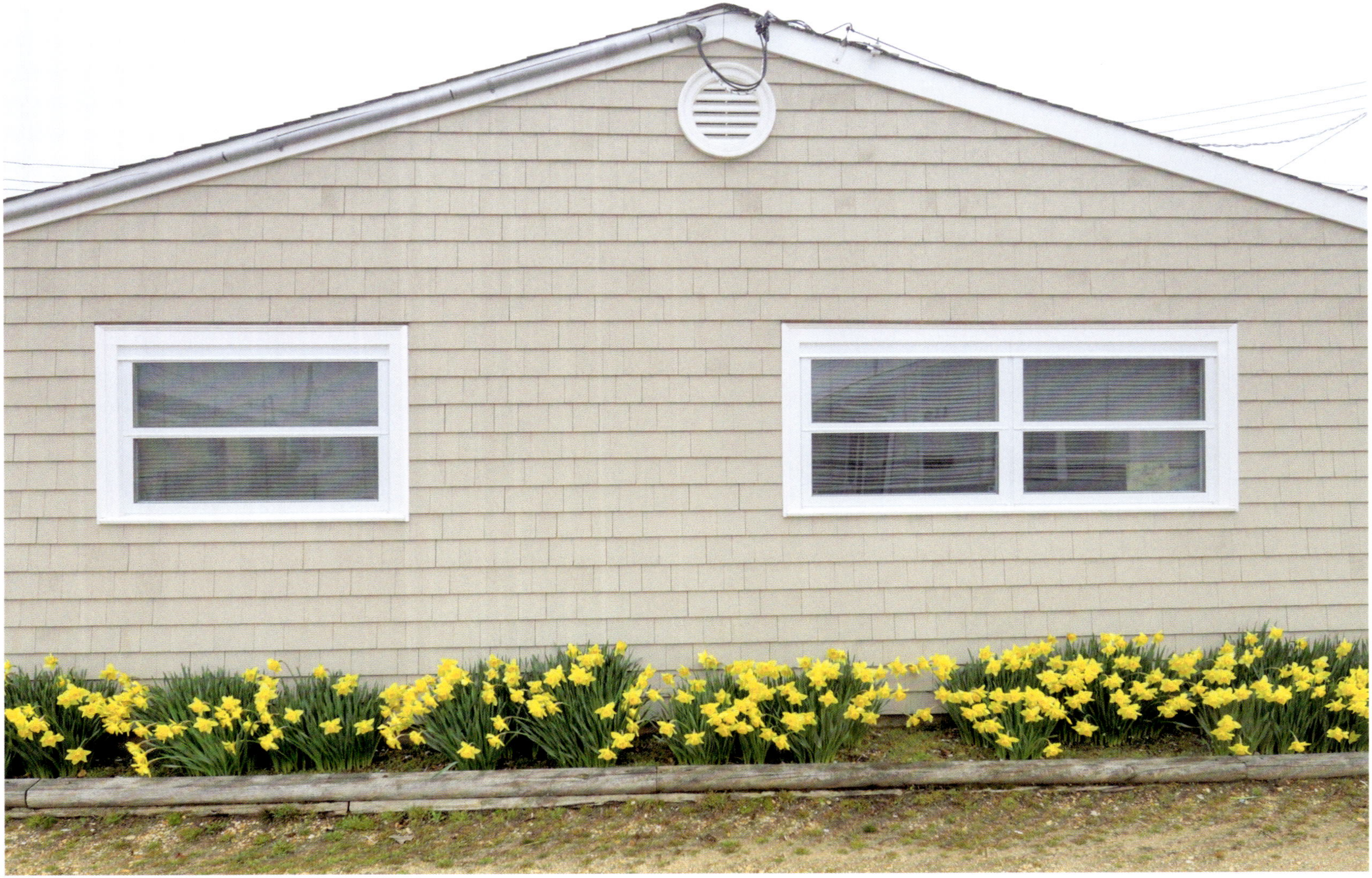

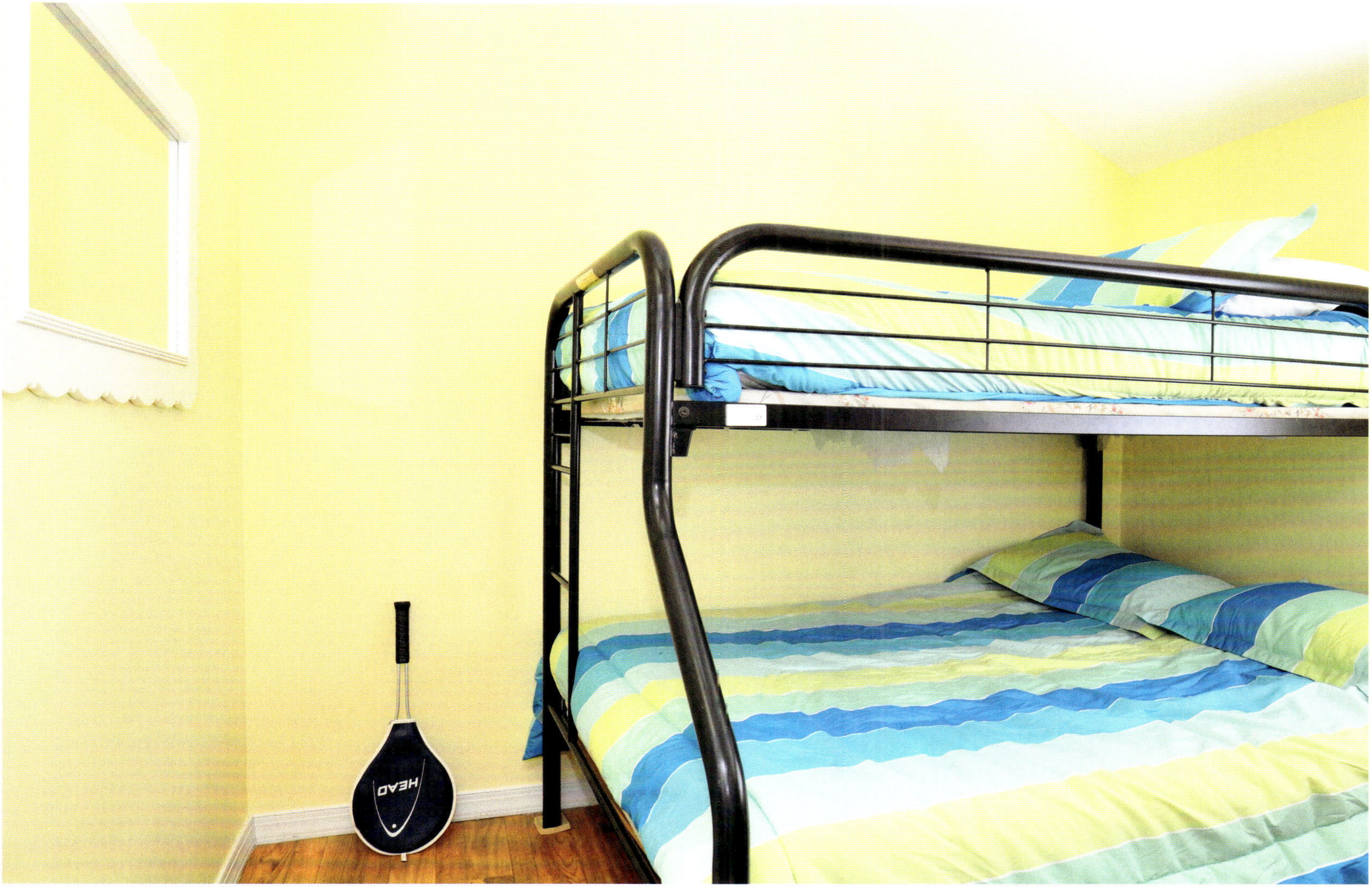

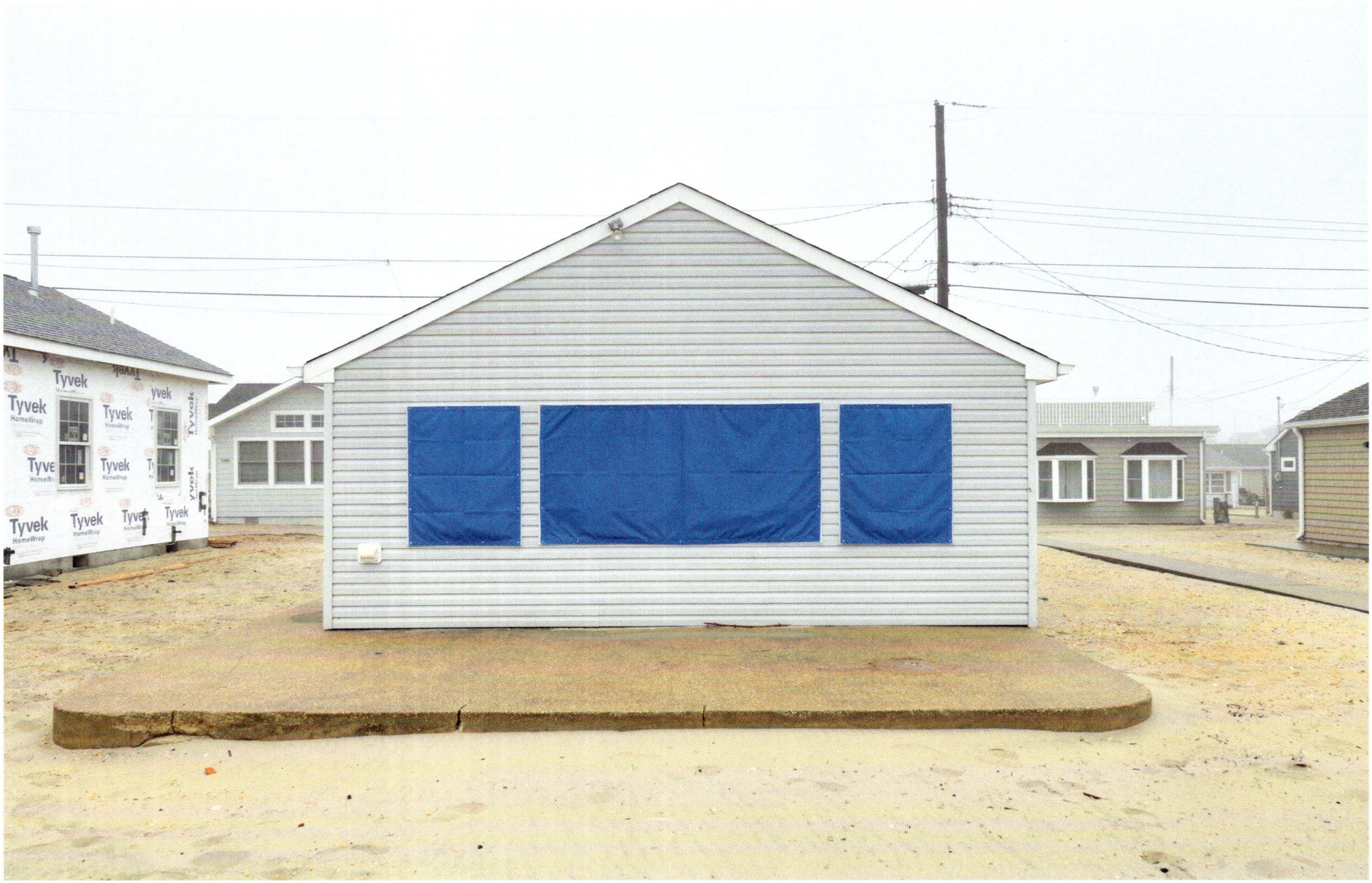
Tyvek
HomeWrap

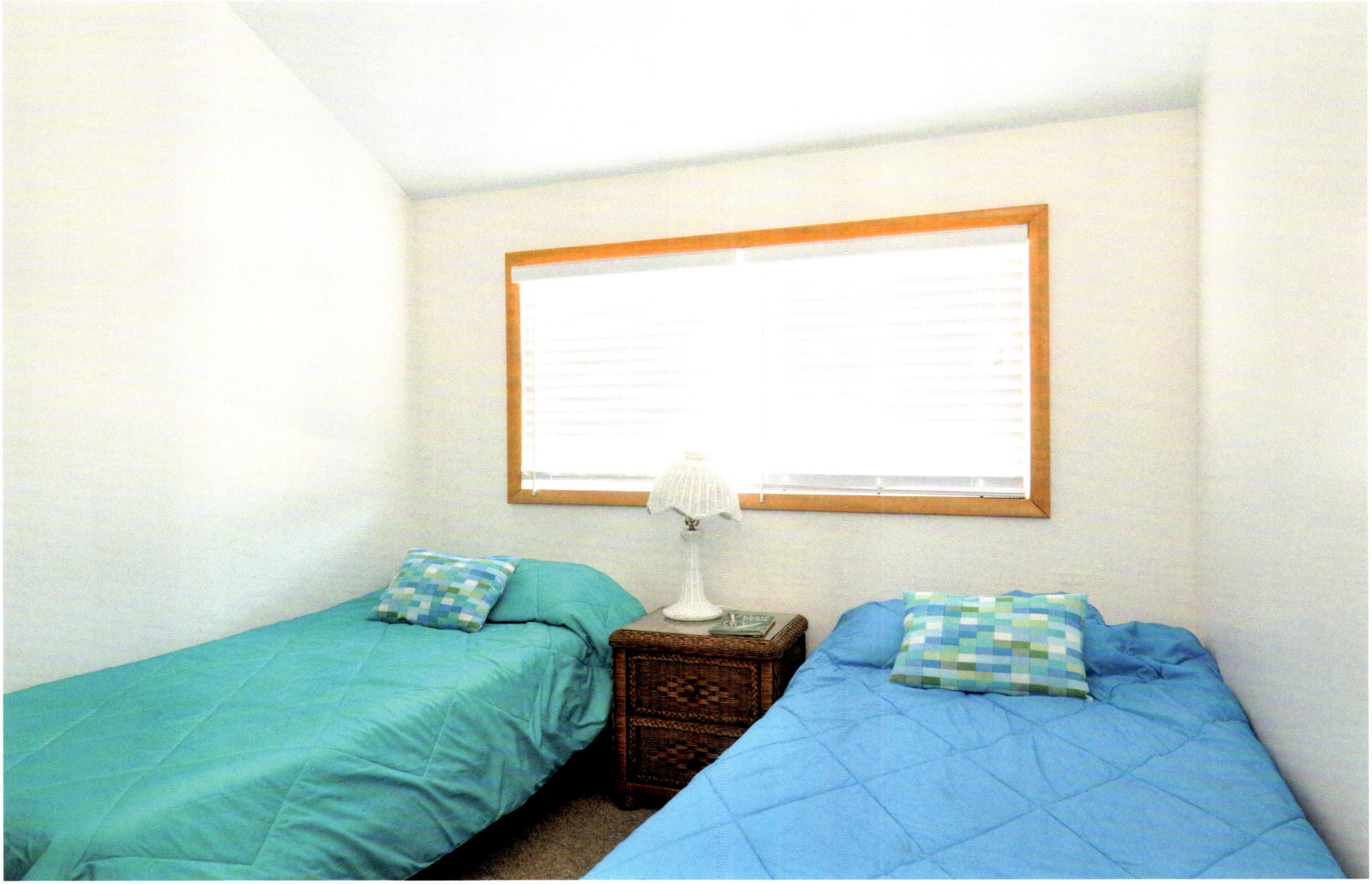

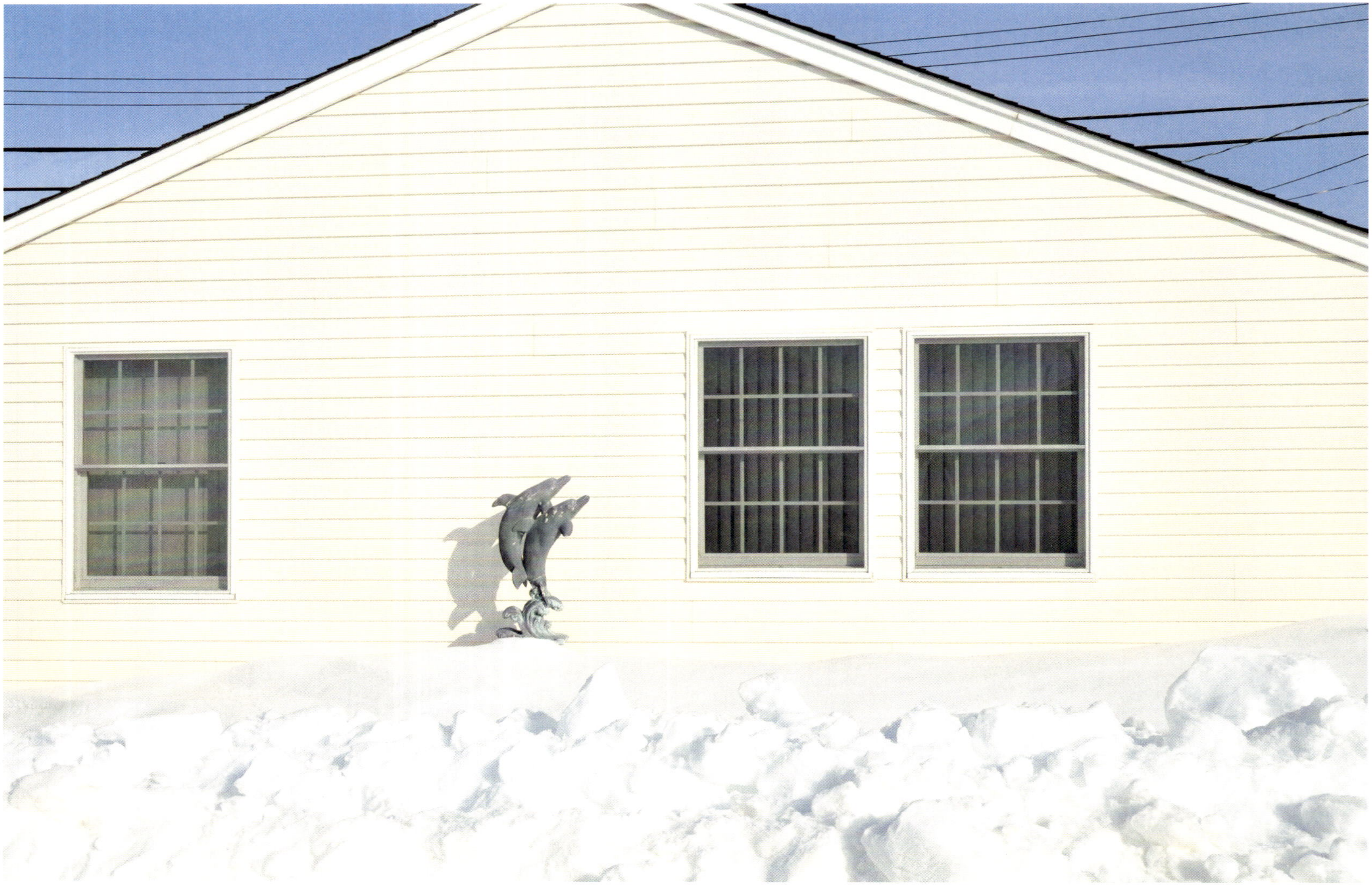

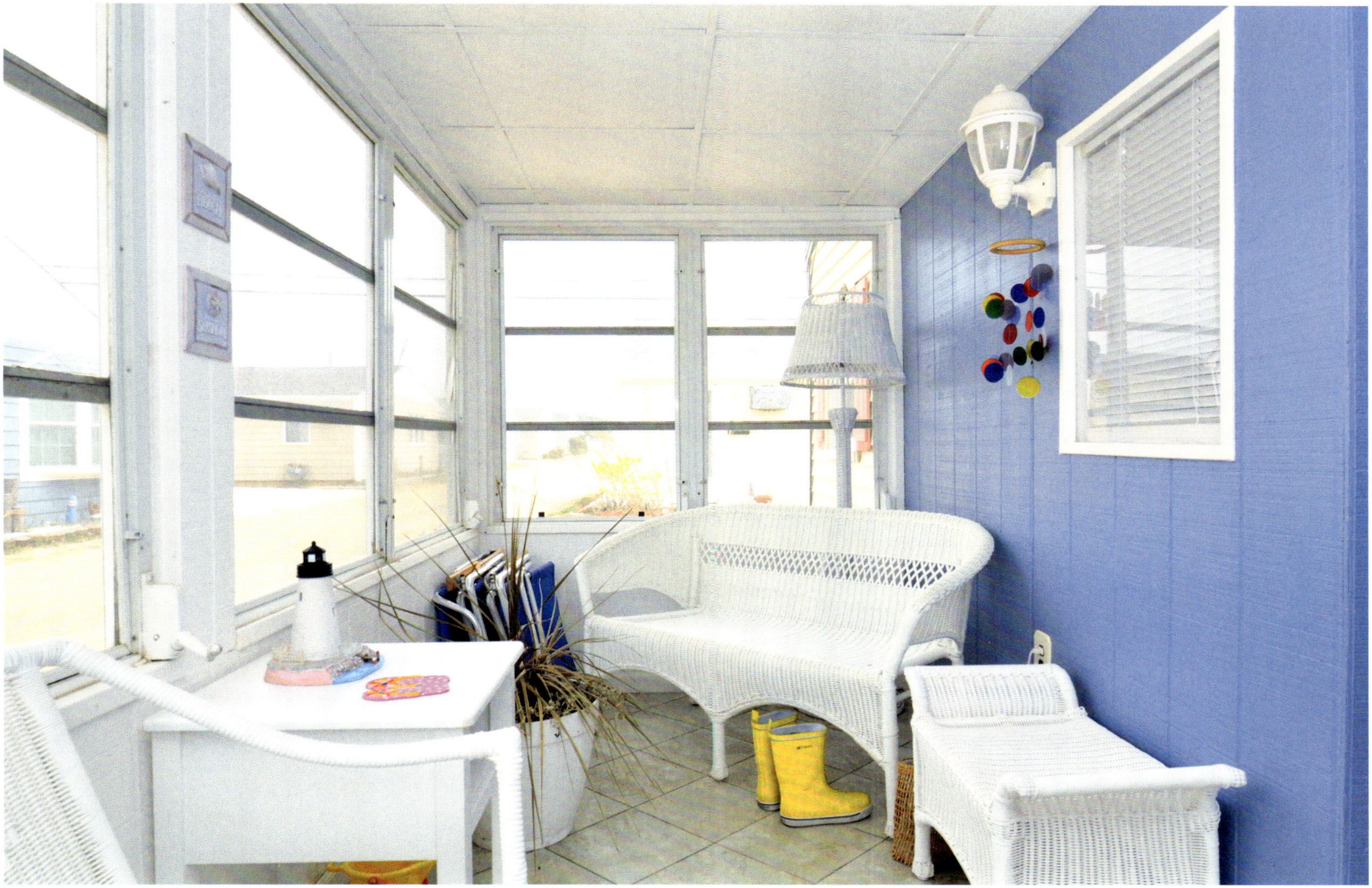

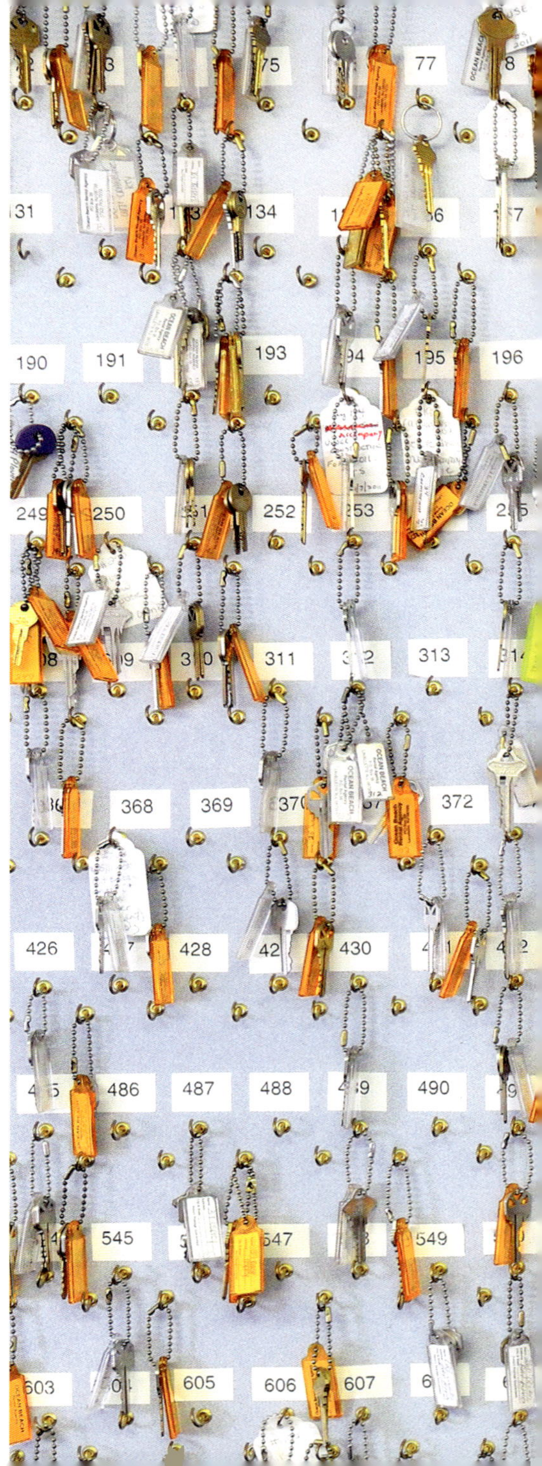
75
77
134
190
191
193
195
196
250
252
253
311
313
368
369
372
426
428
430
486
487
488
490
545
547
549
605
606
607

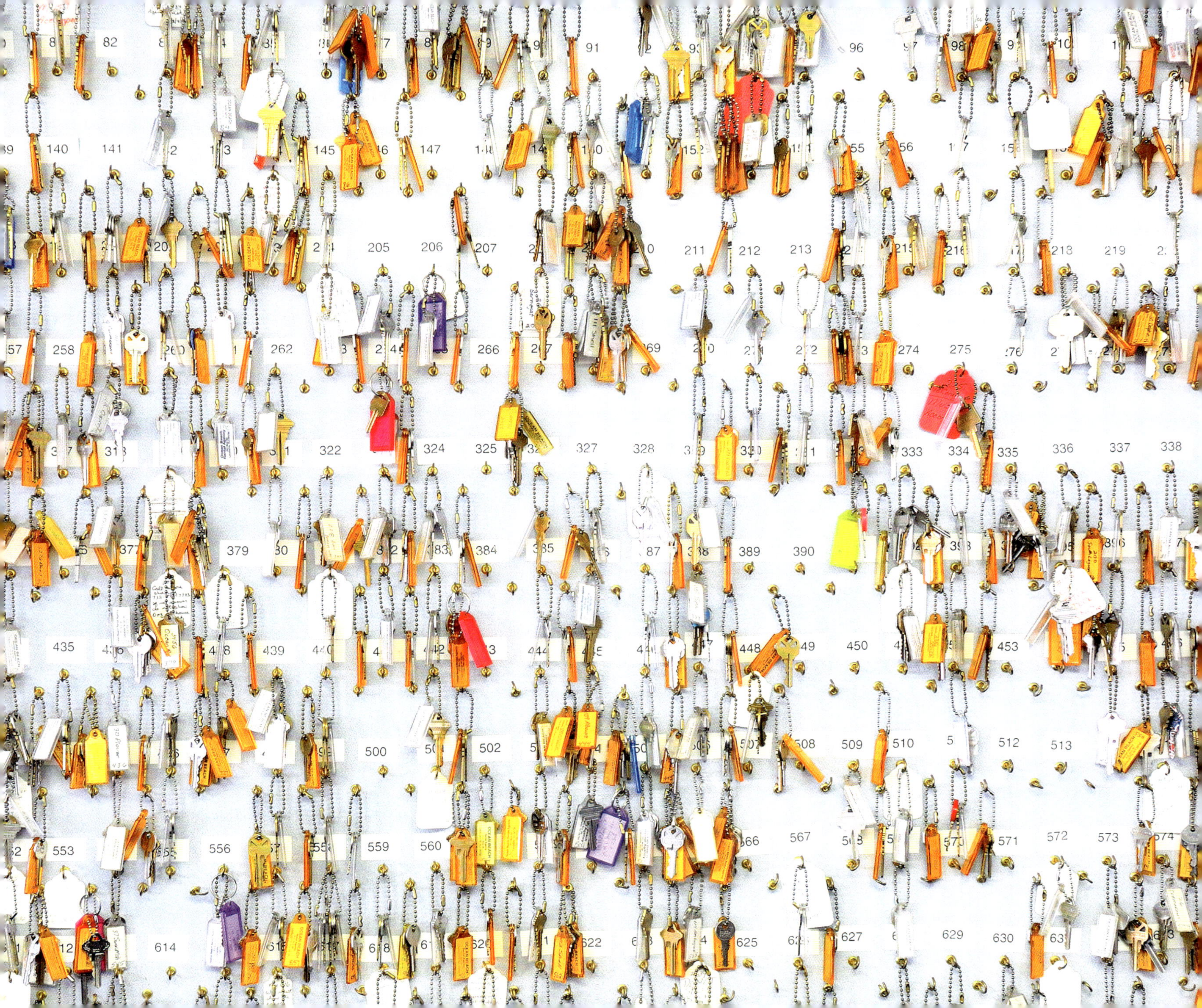

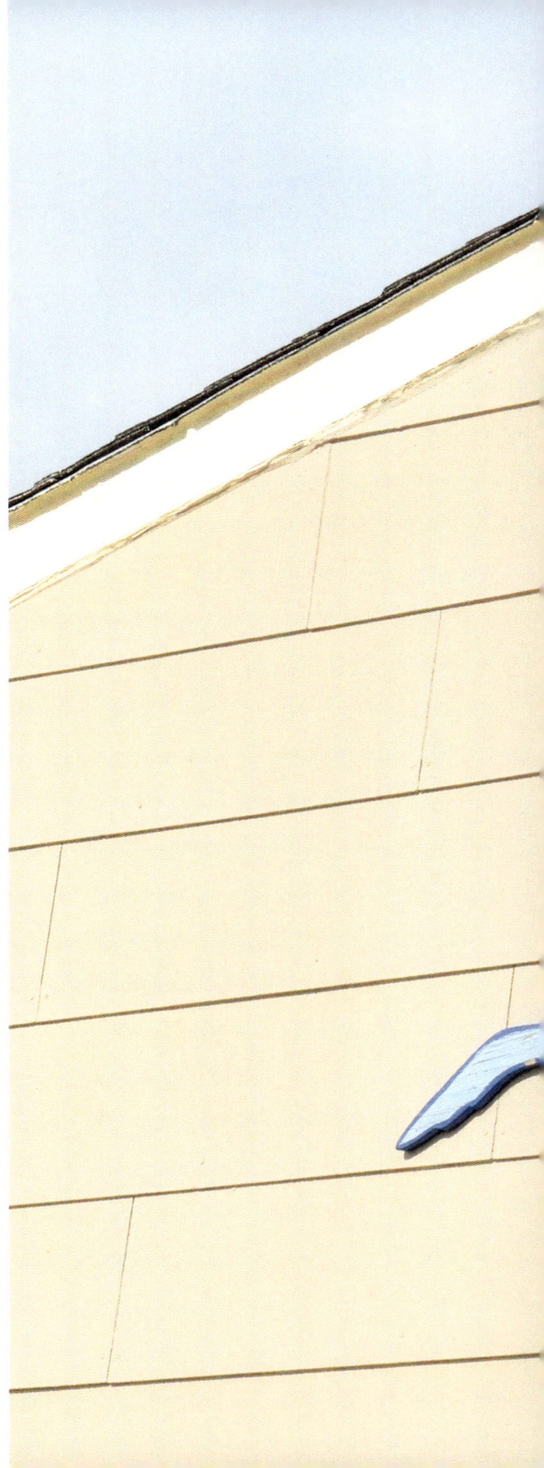

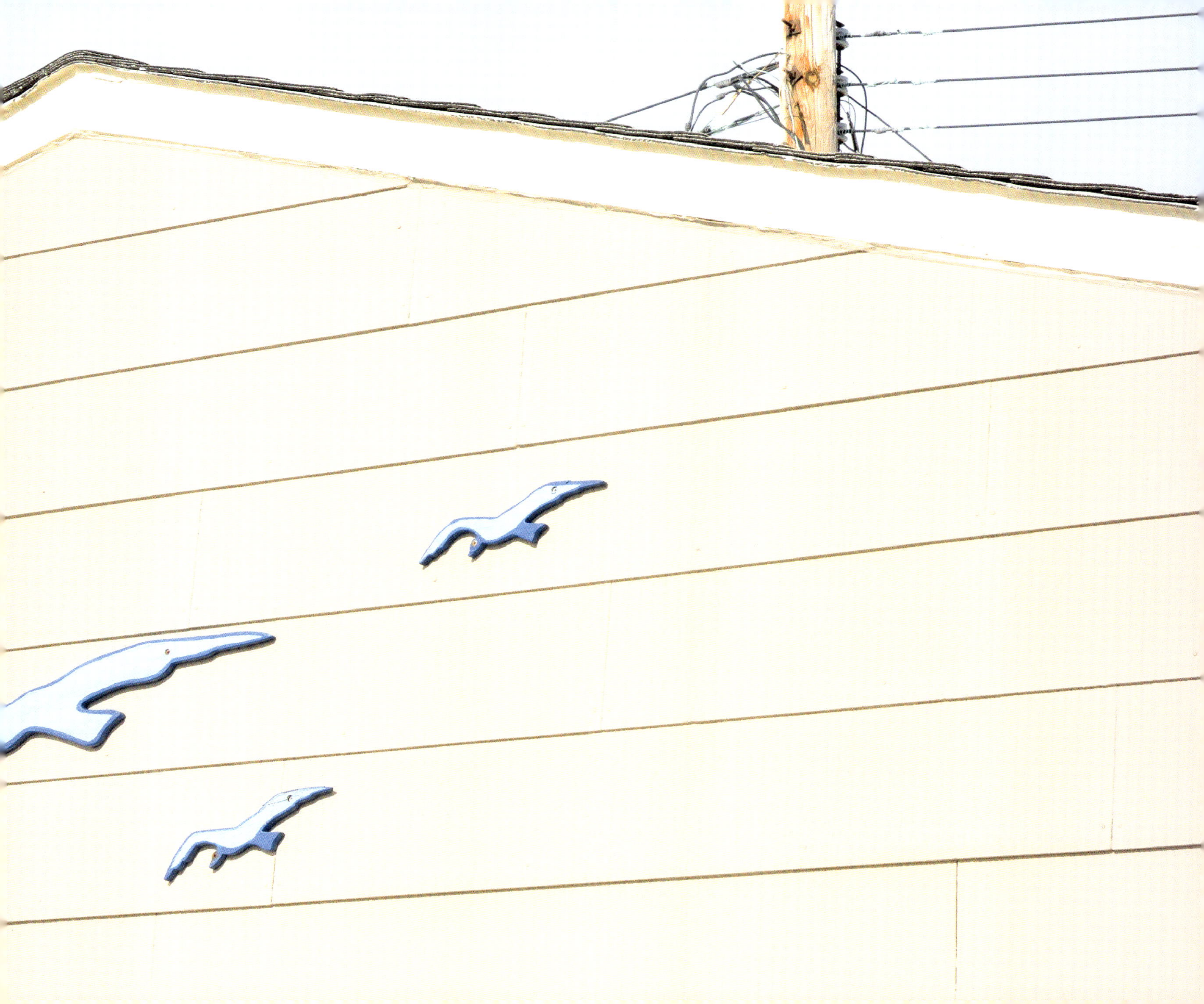

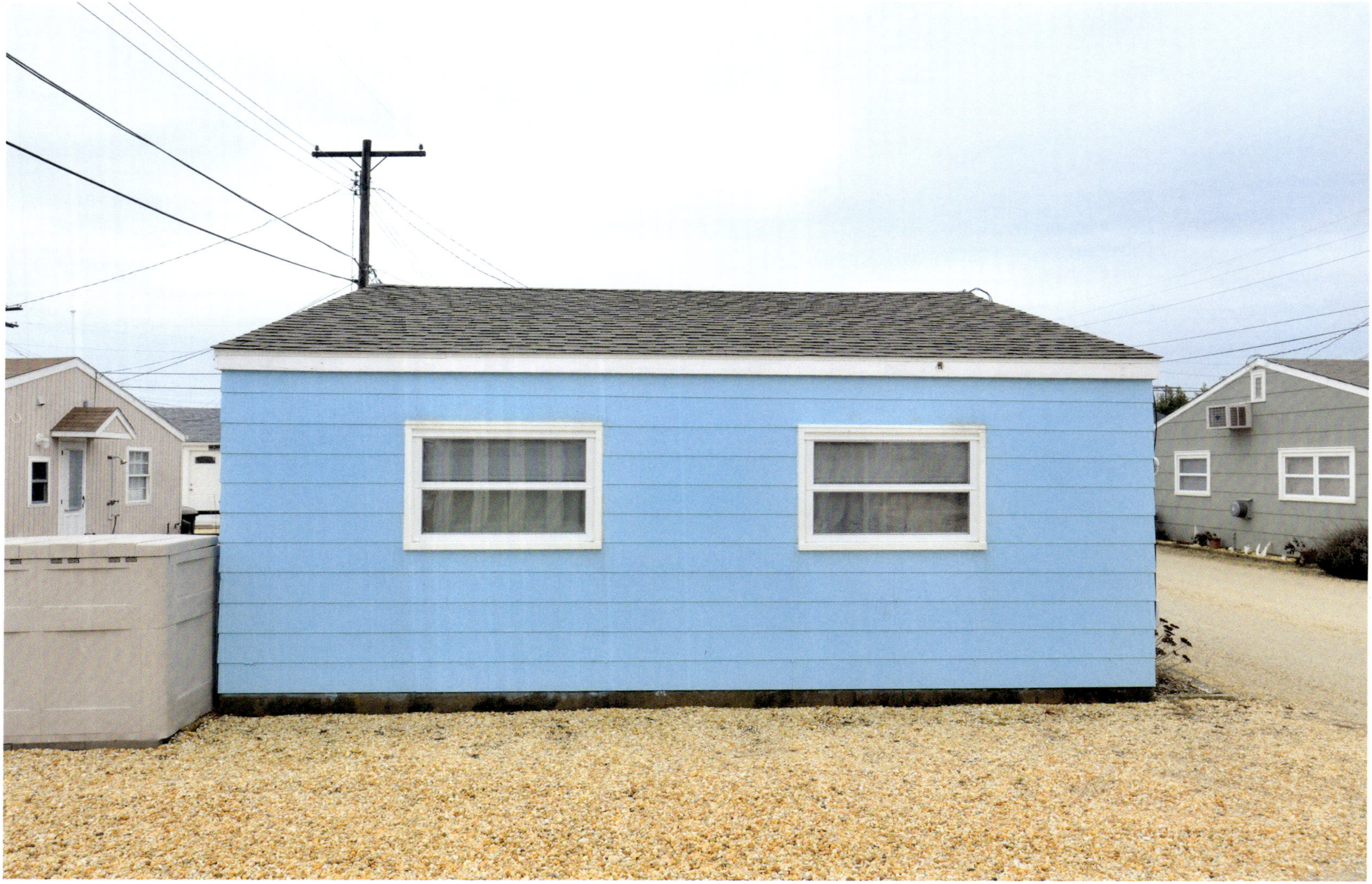

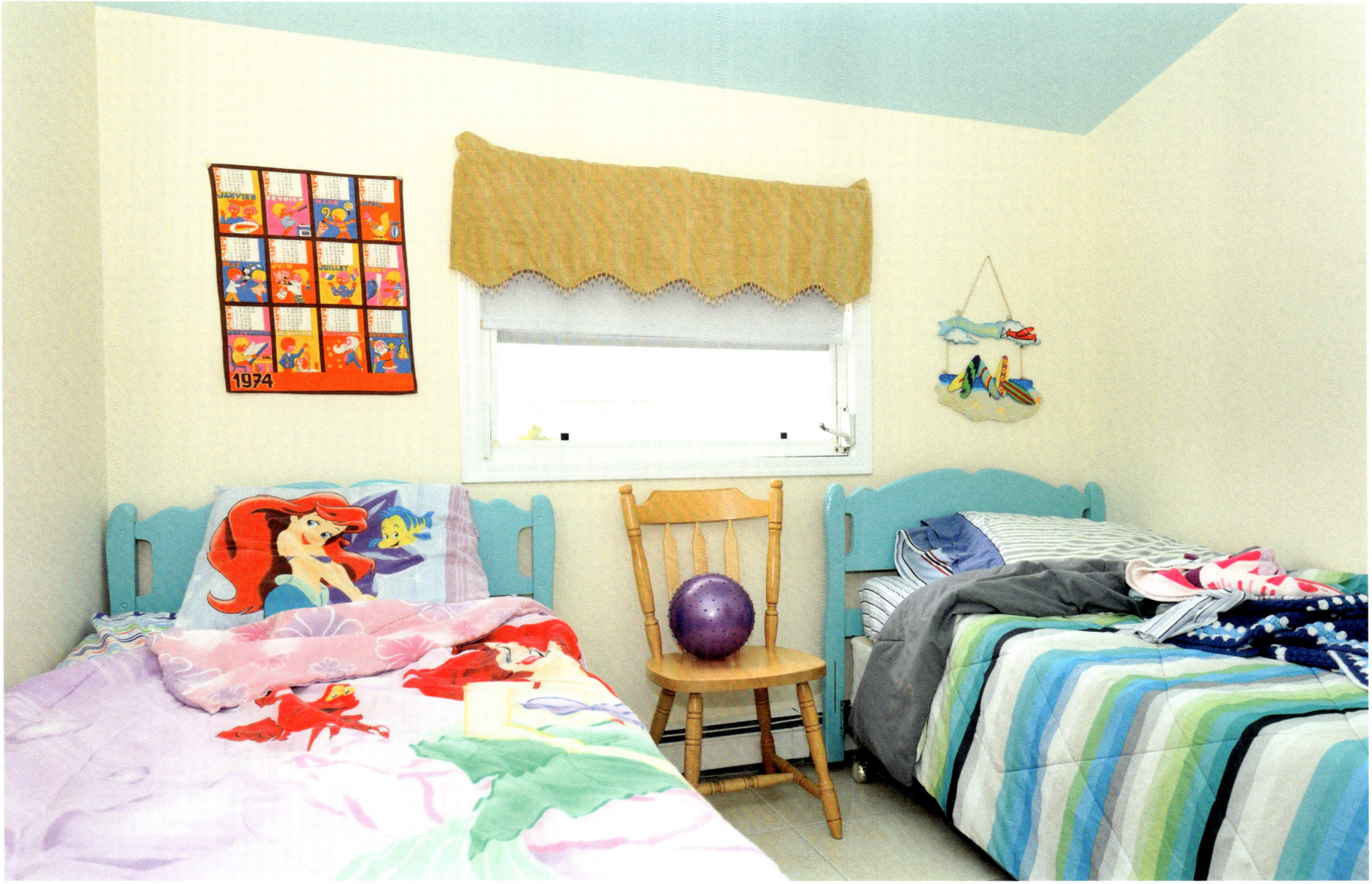
1974

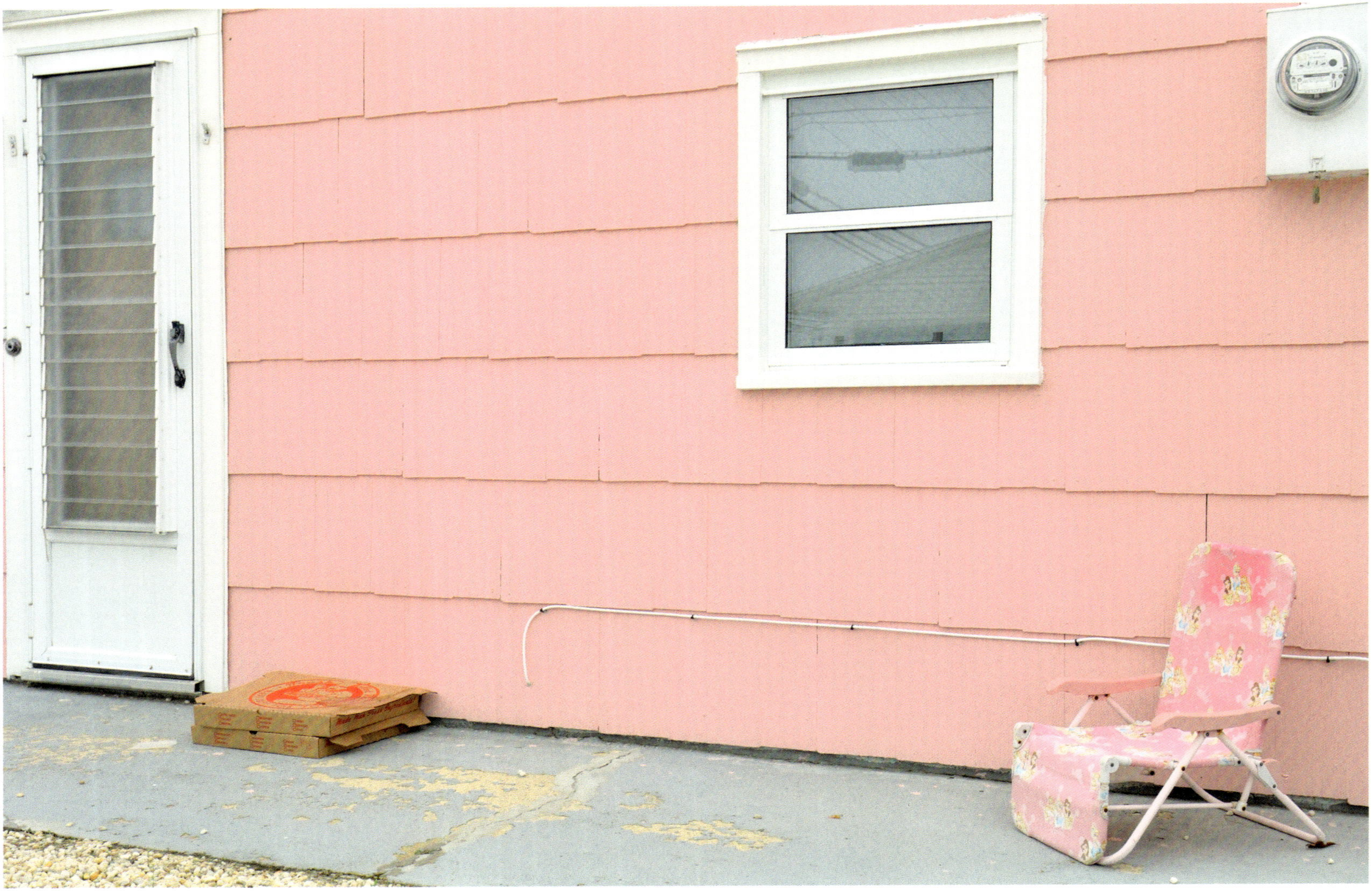

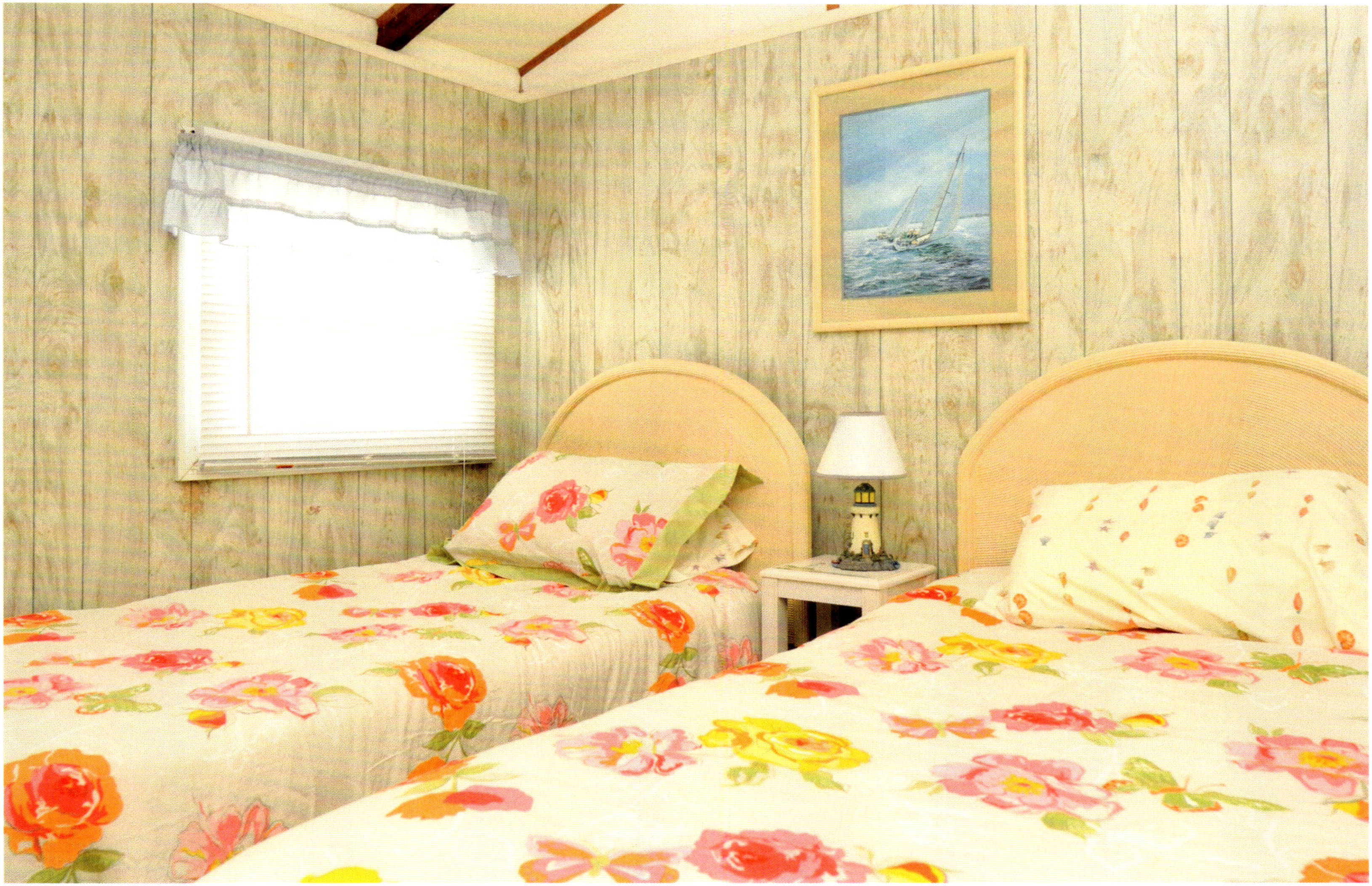

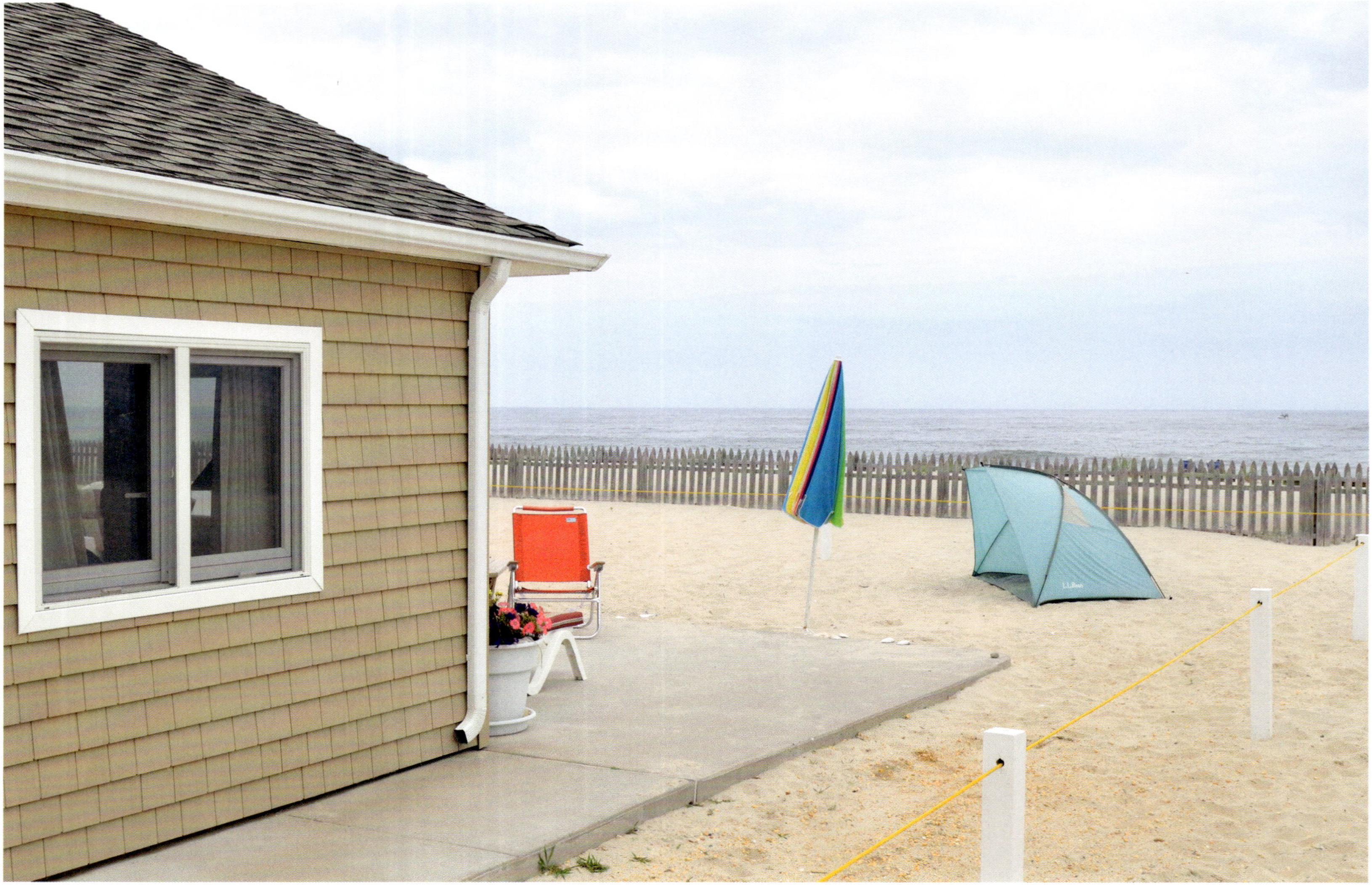

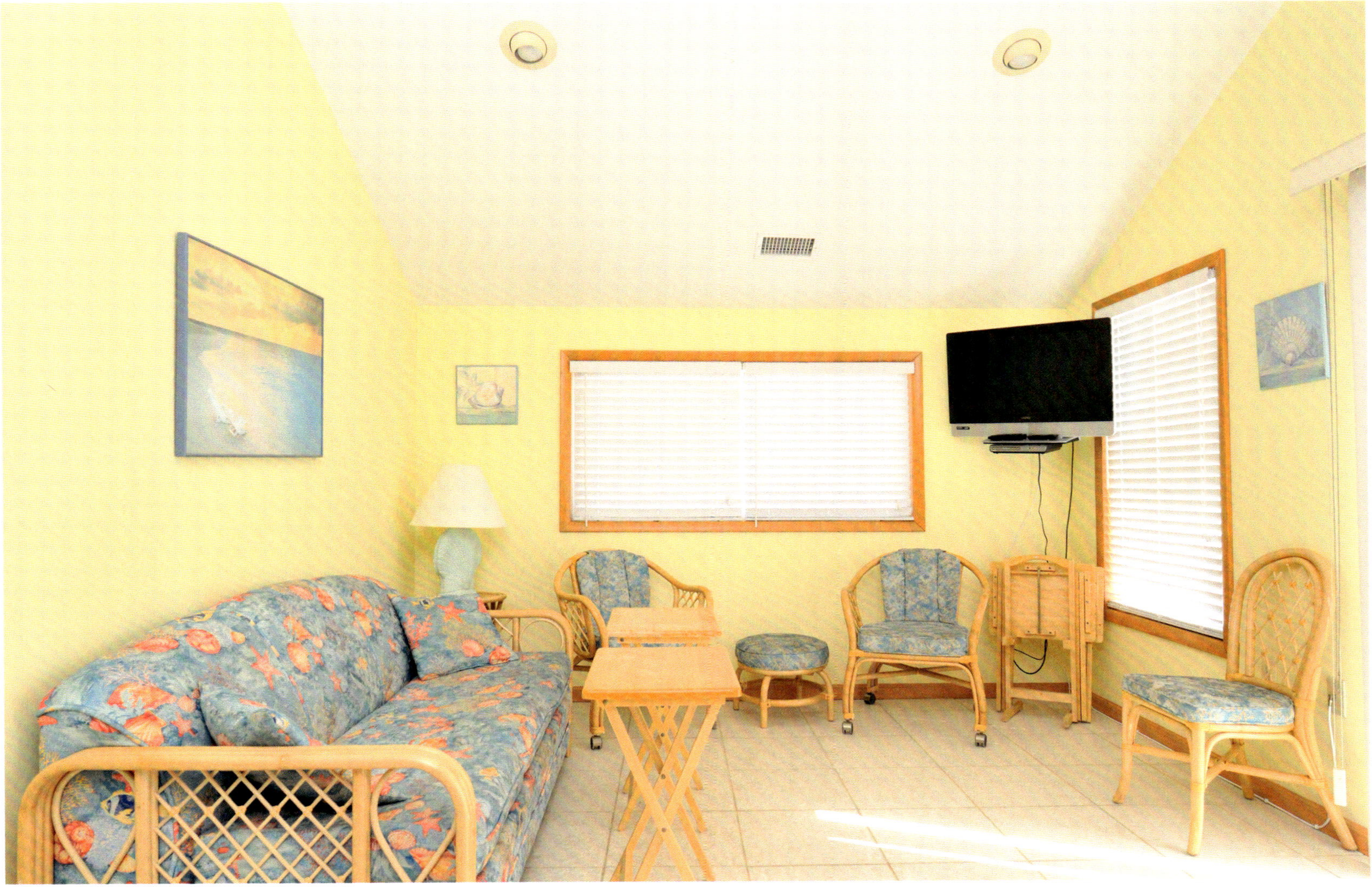

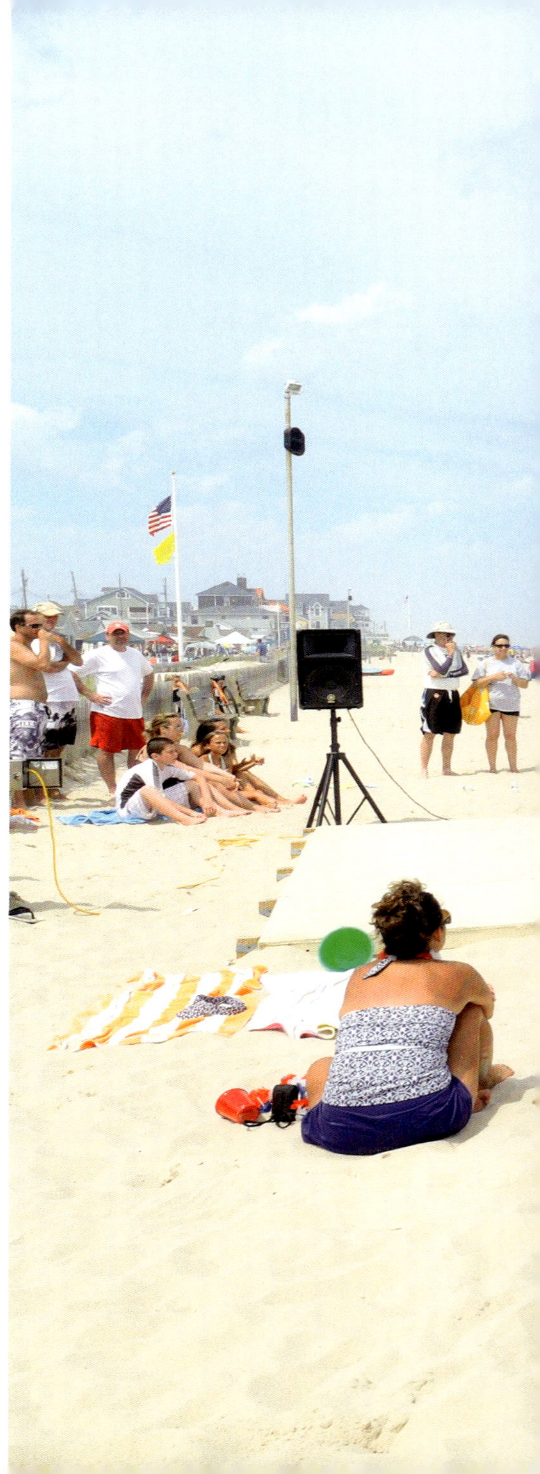

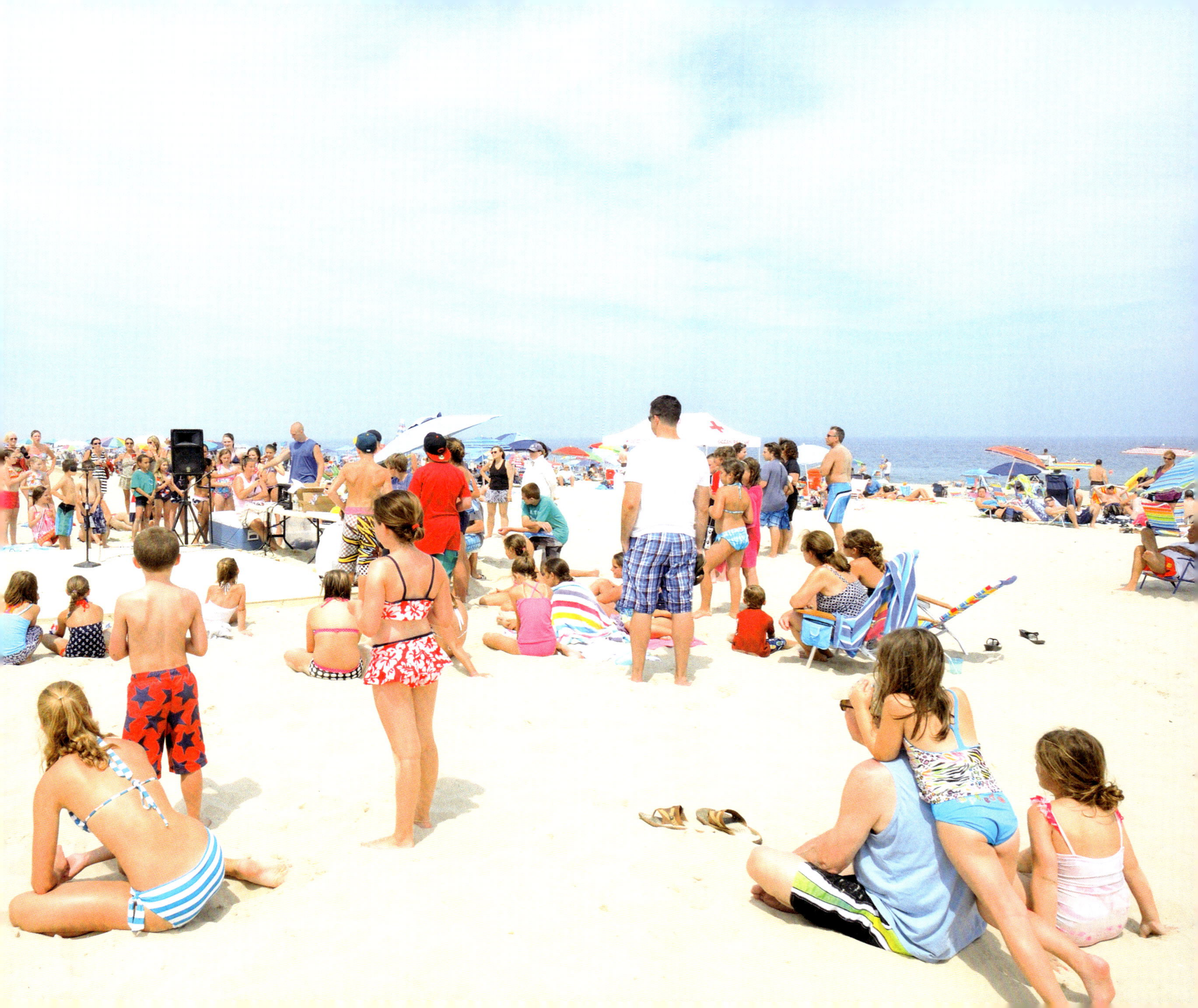

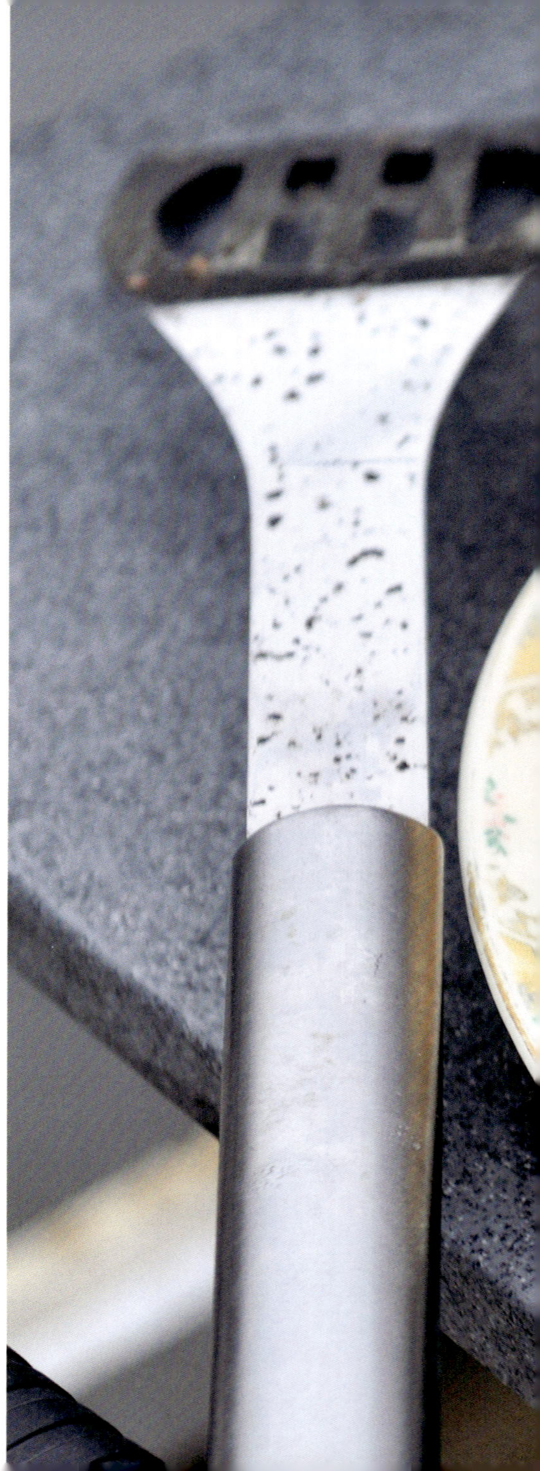

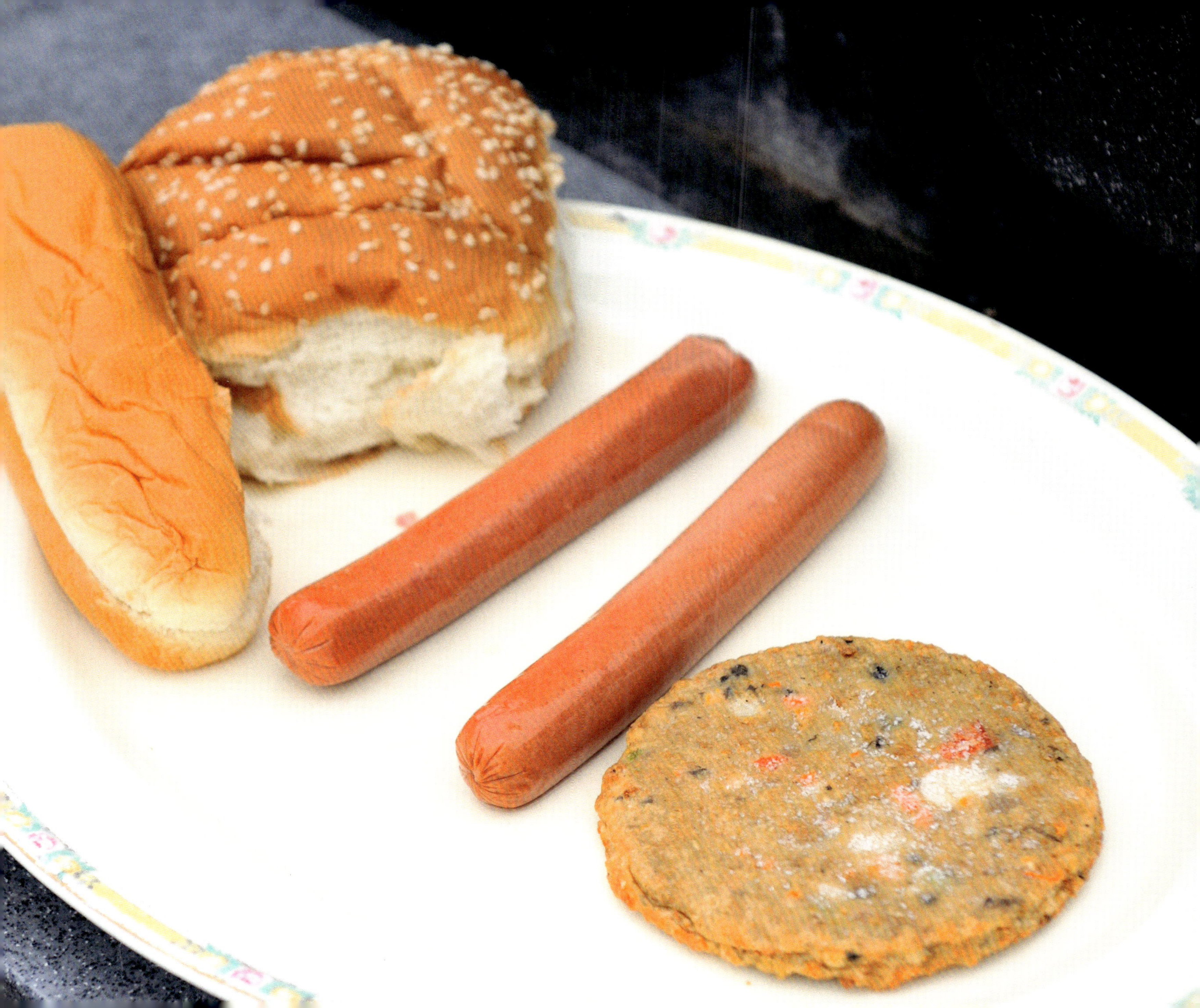

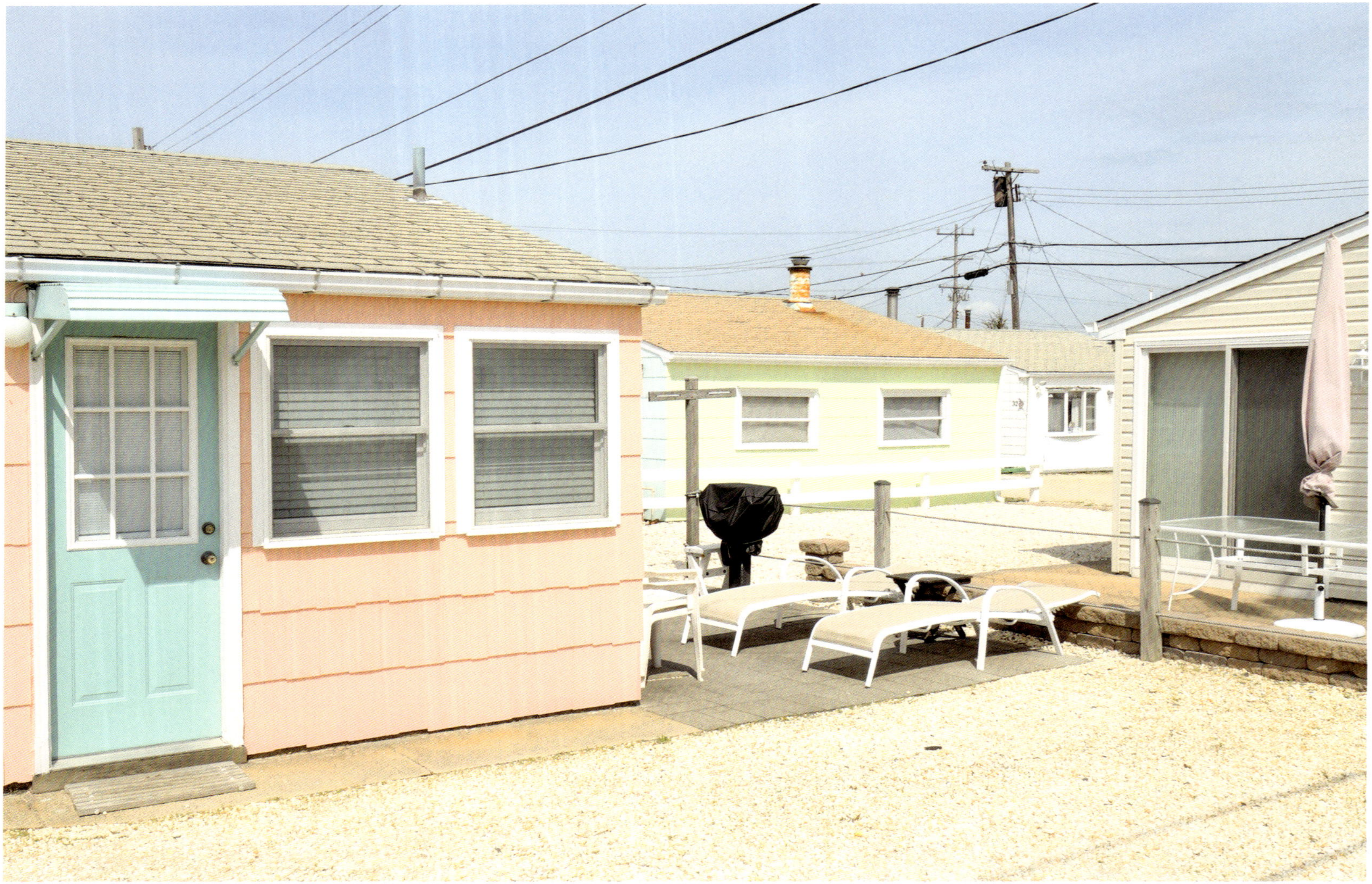

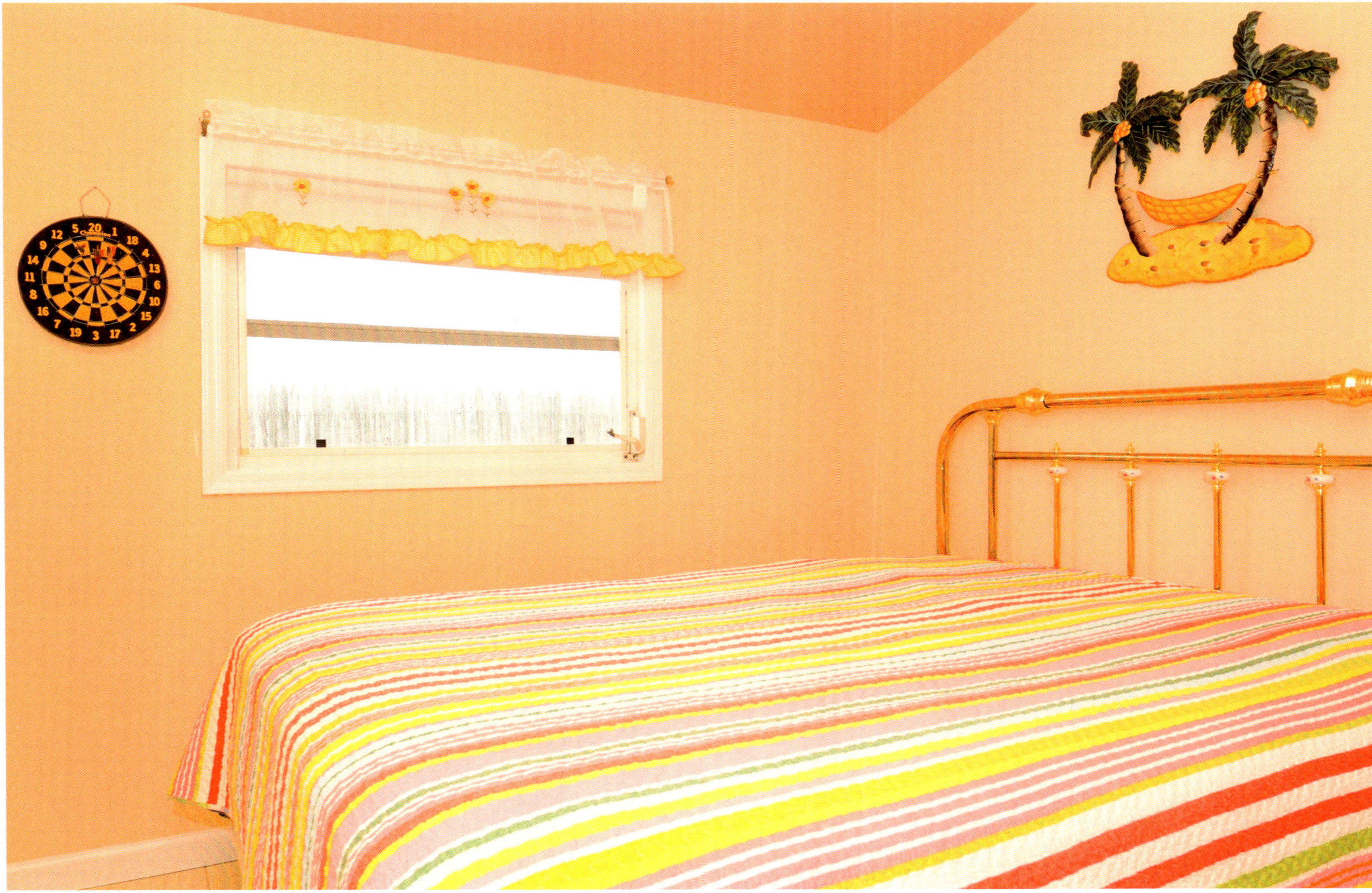

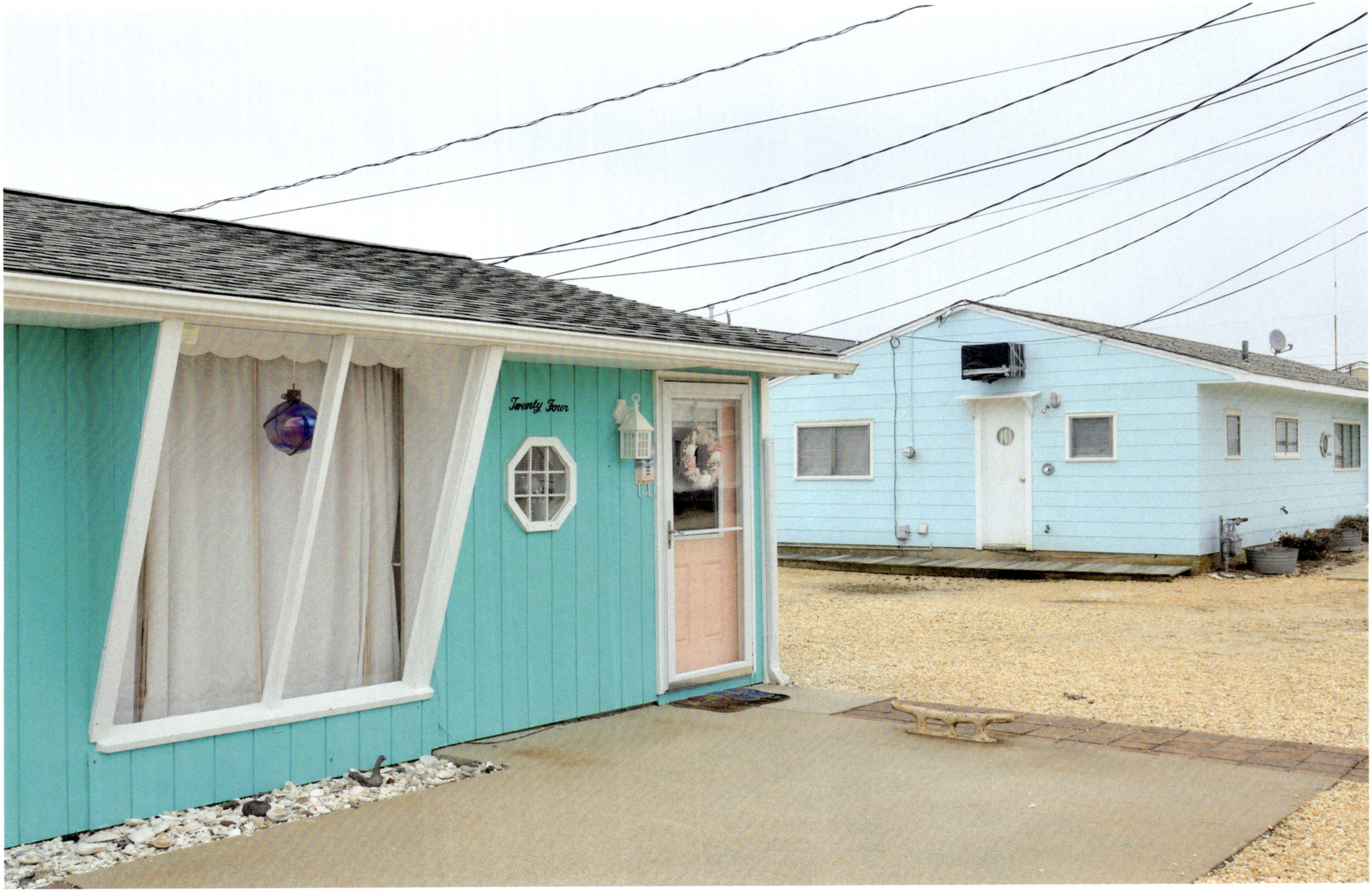
Twenty Four

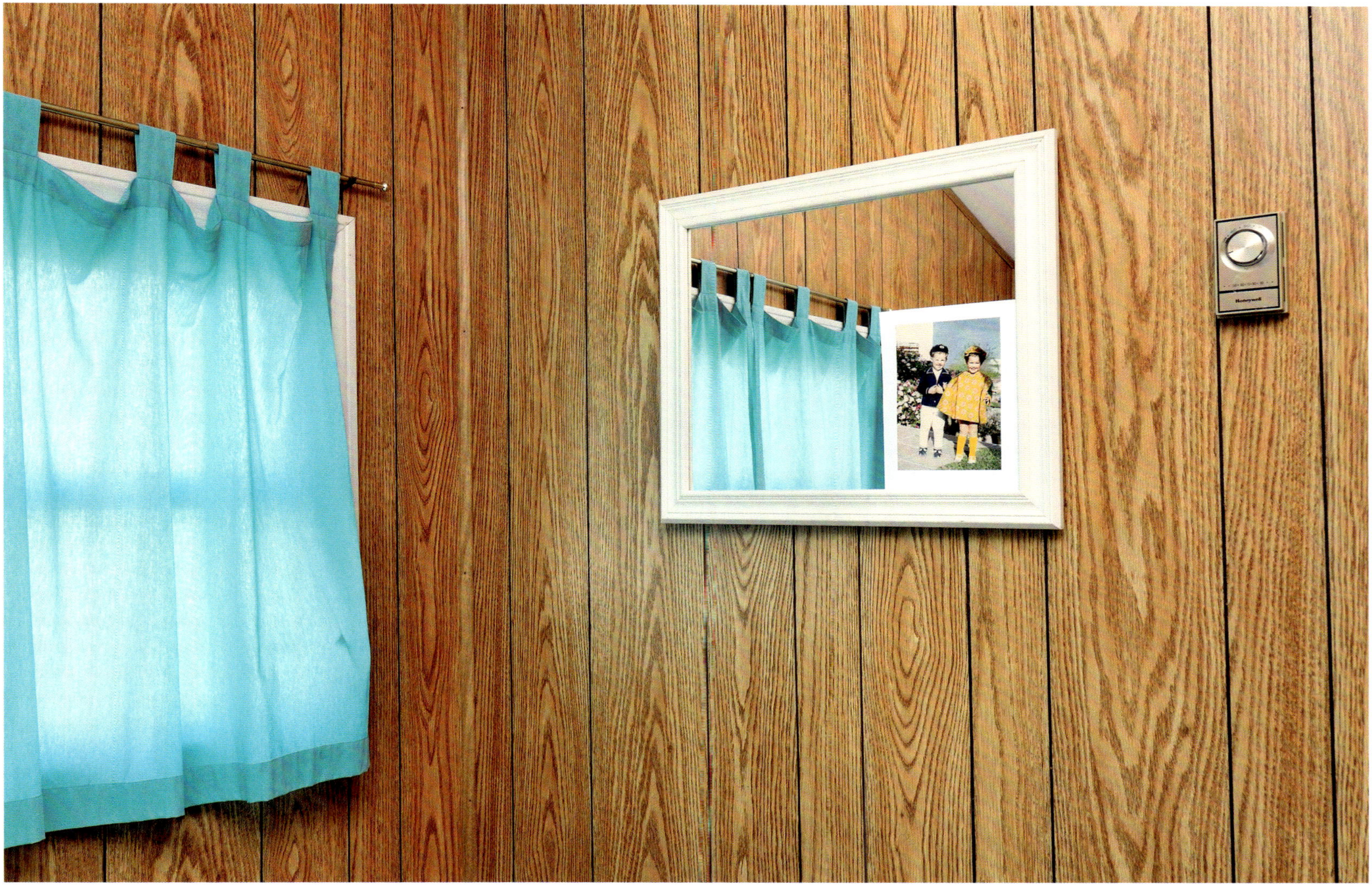

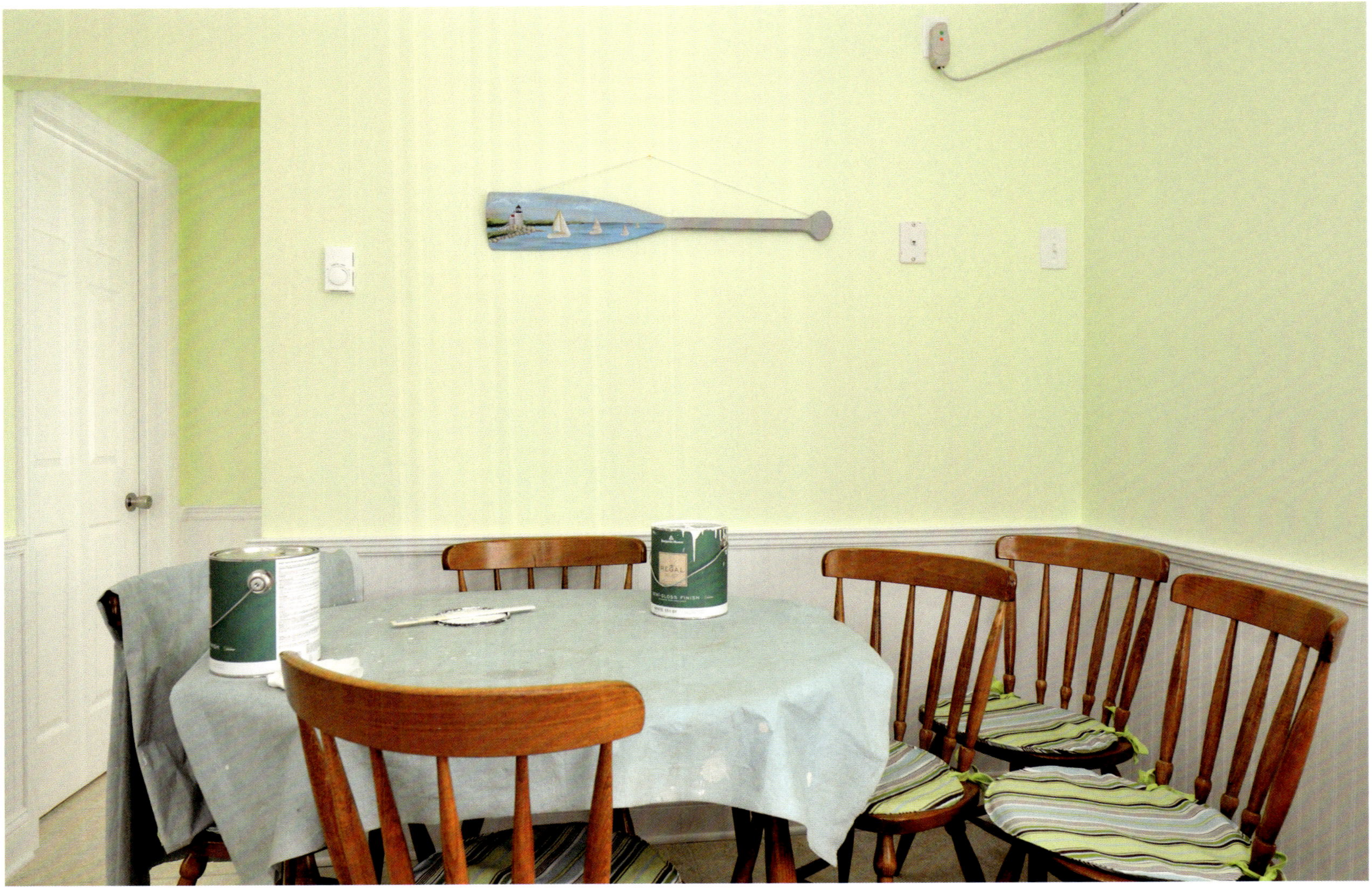

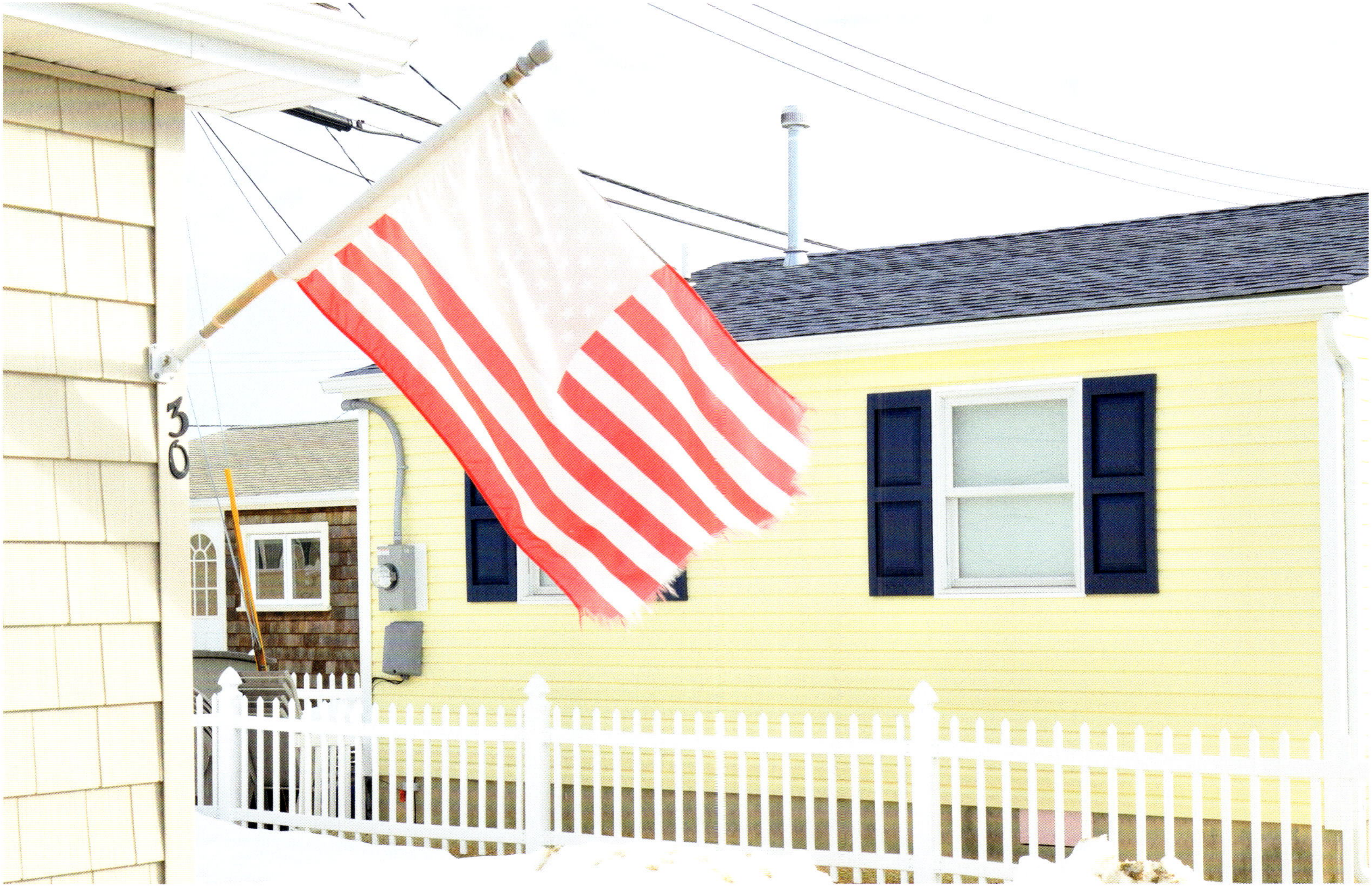
30

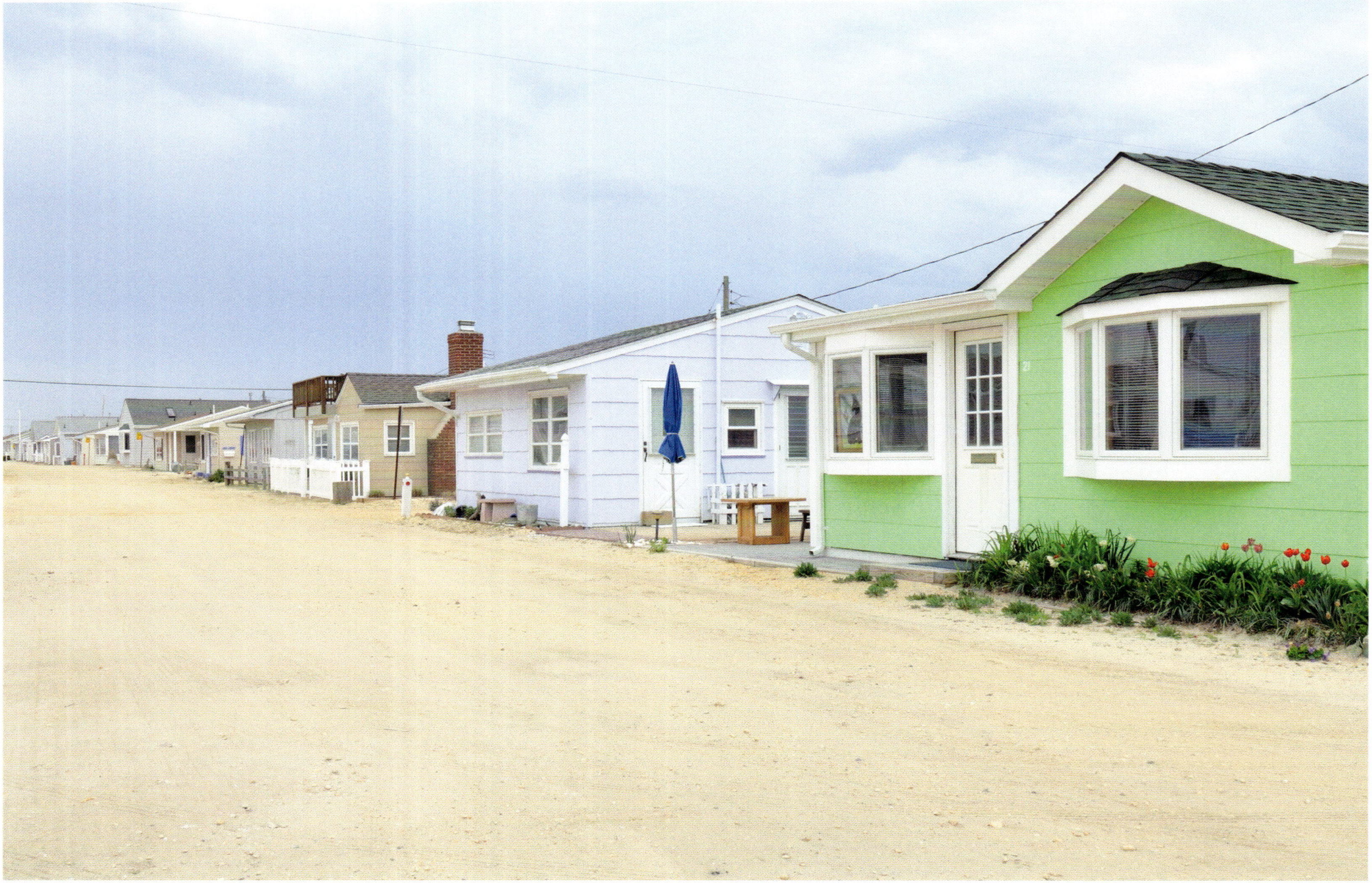

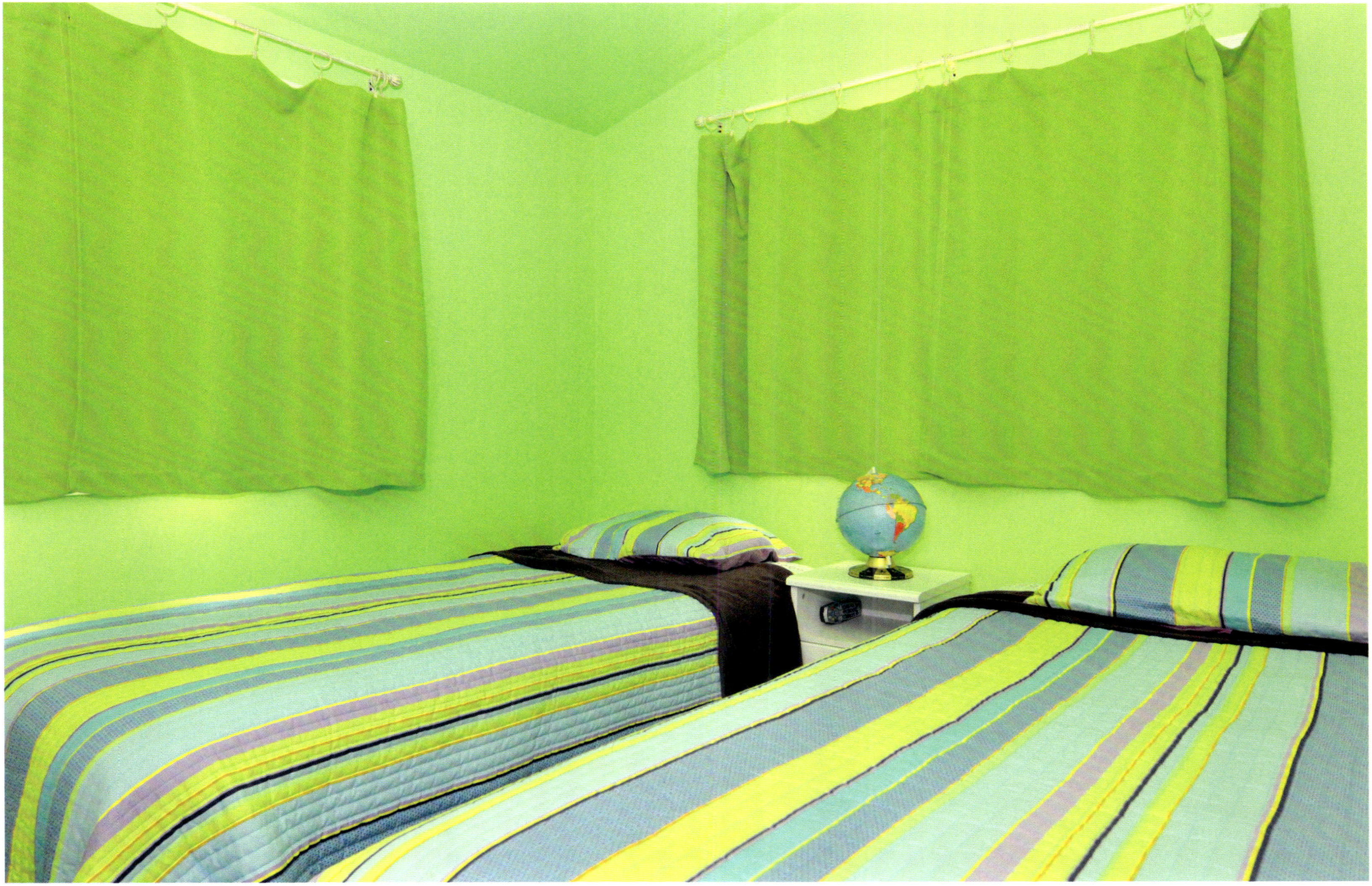

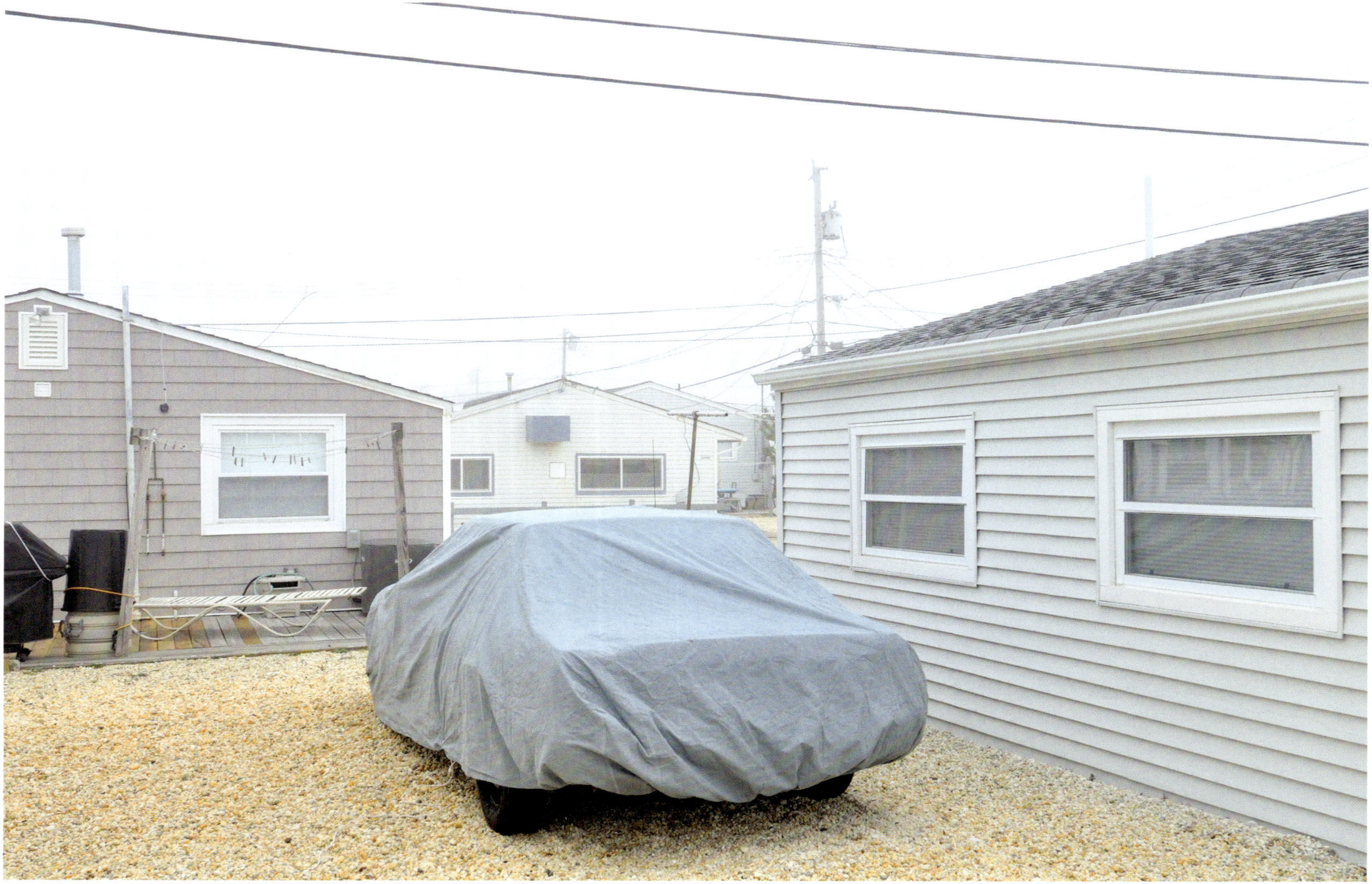

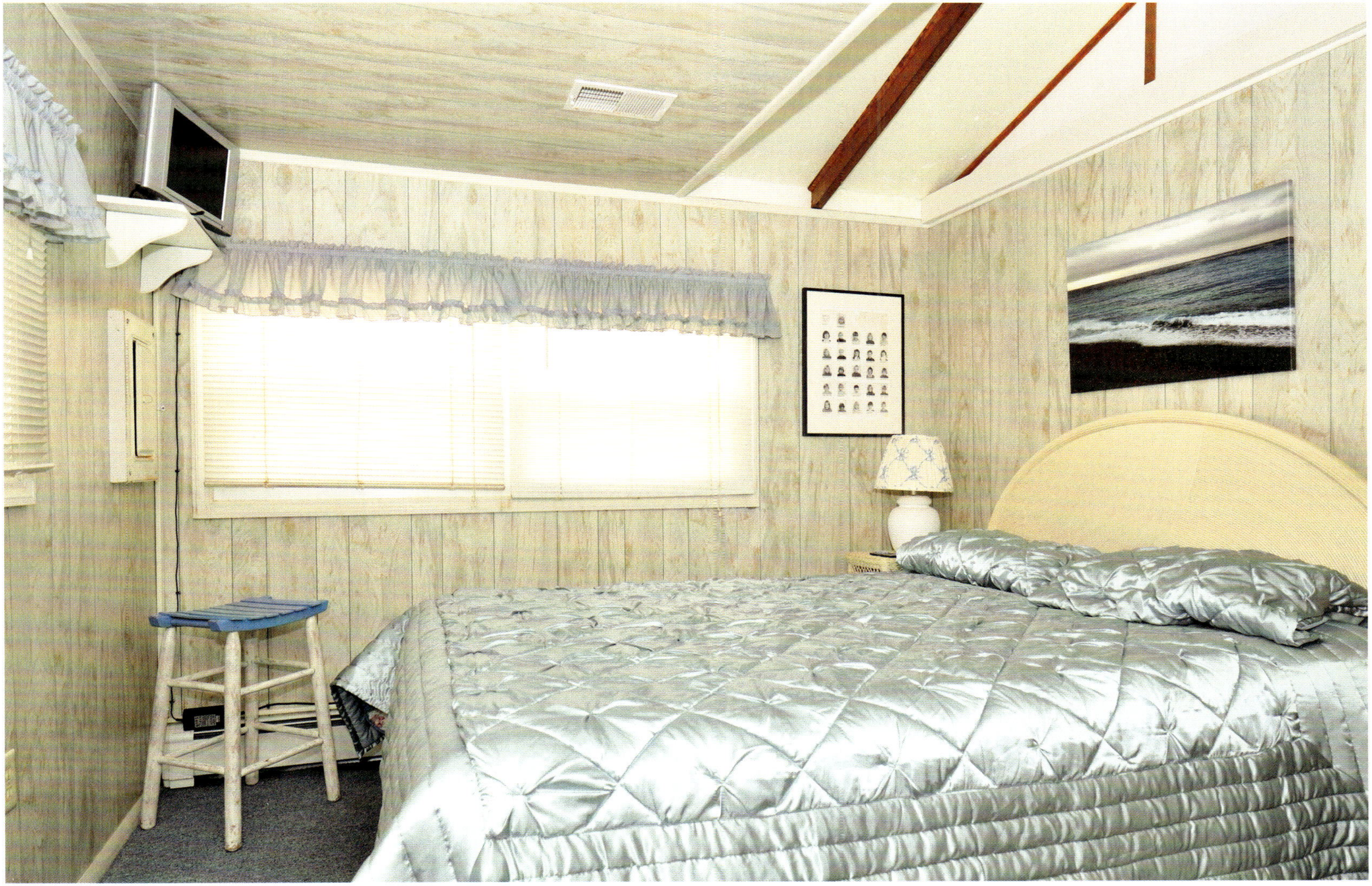

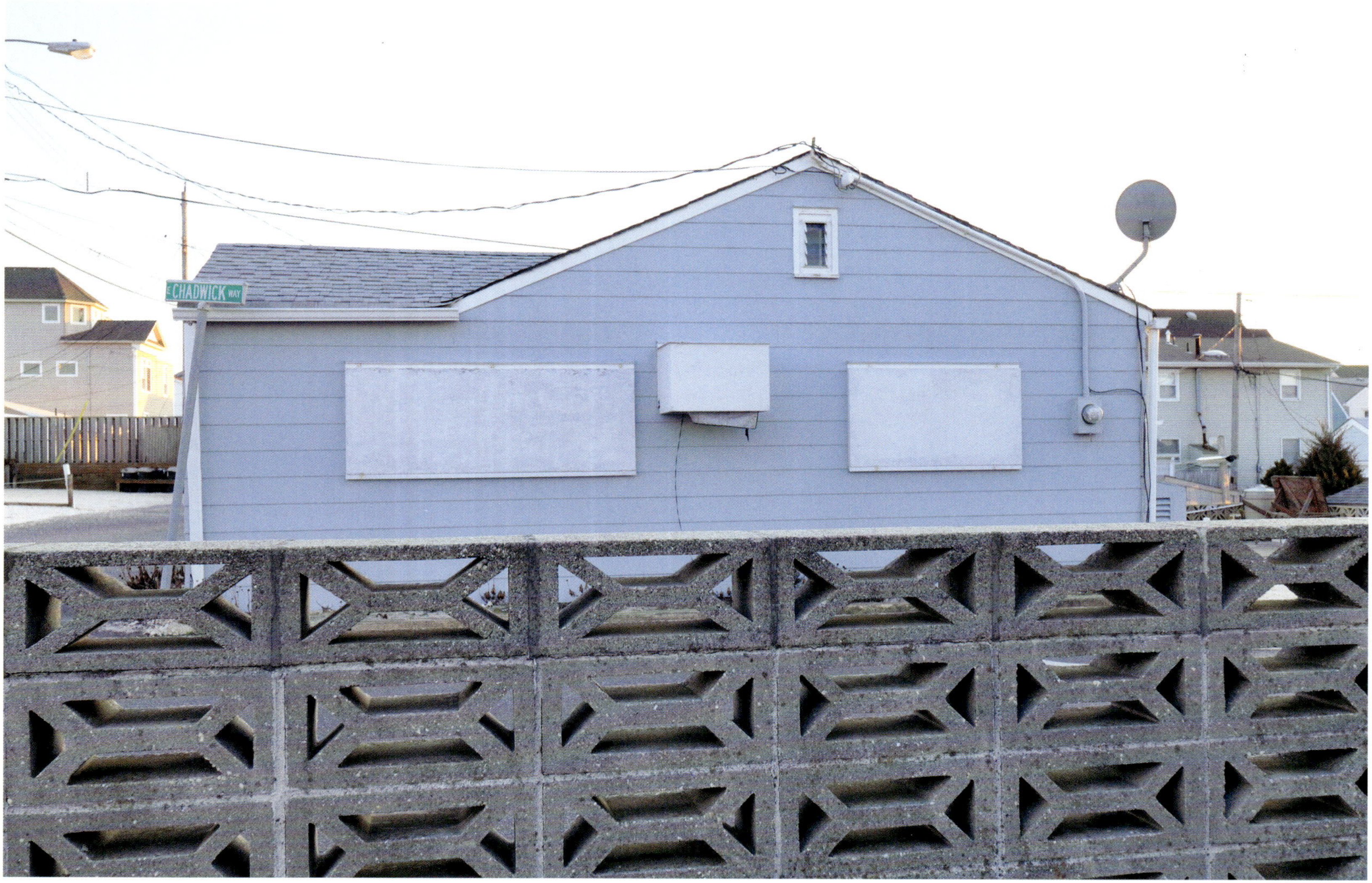
E CHADWICK WAY

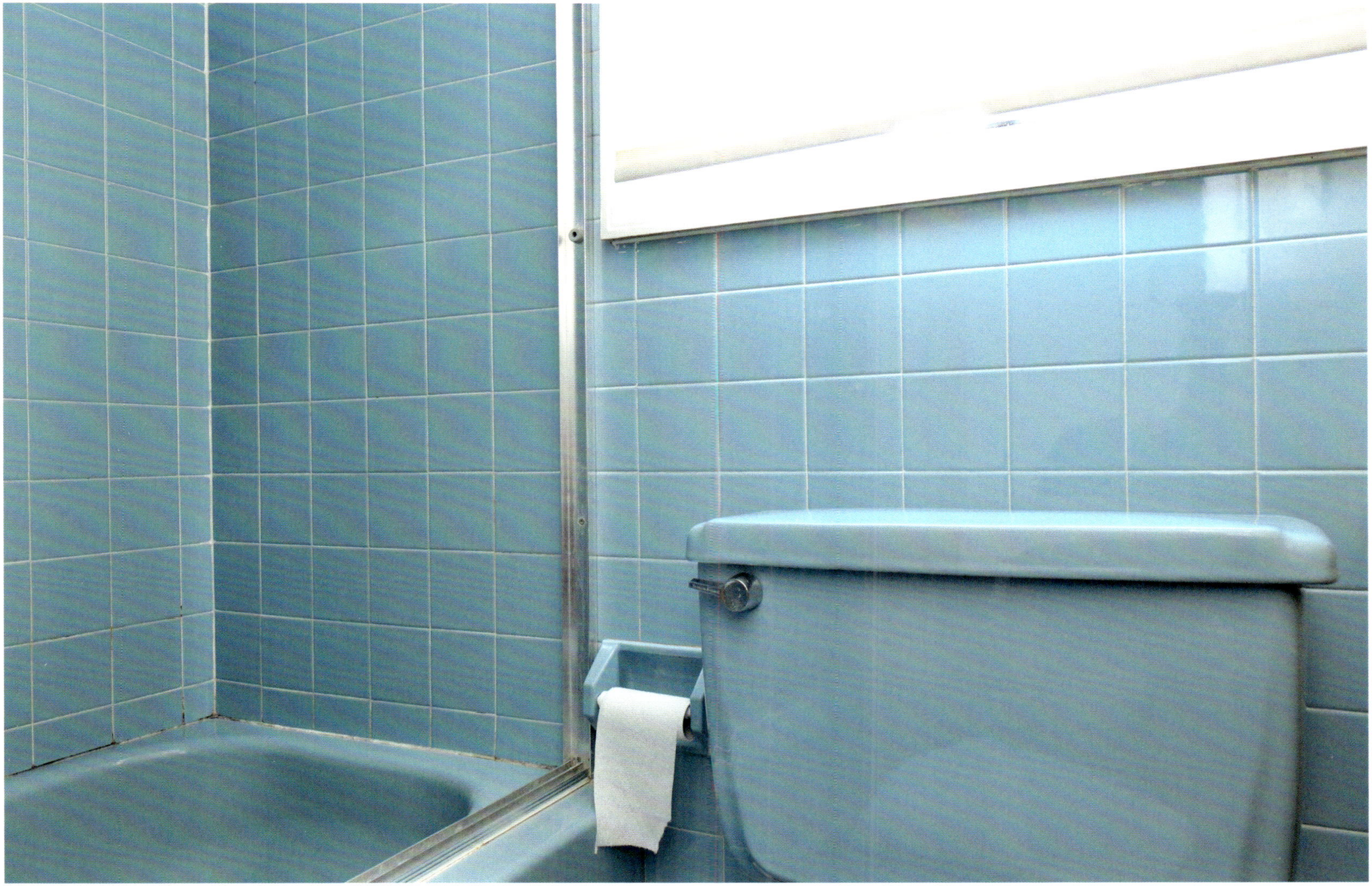

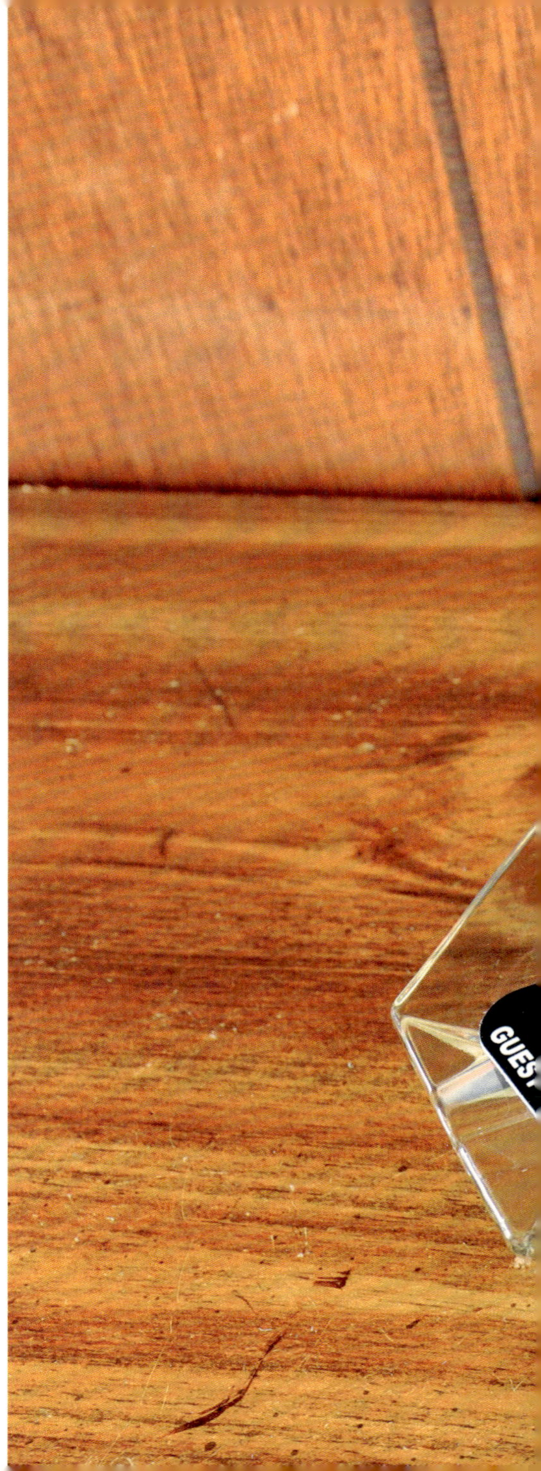

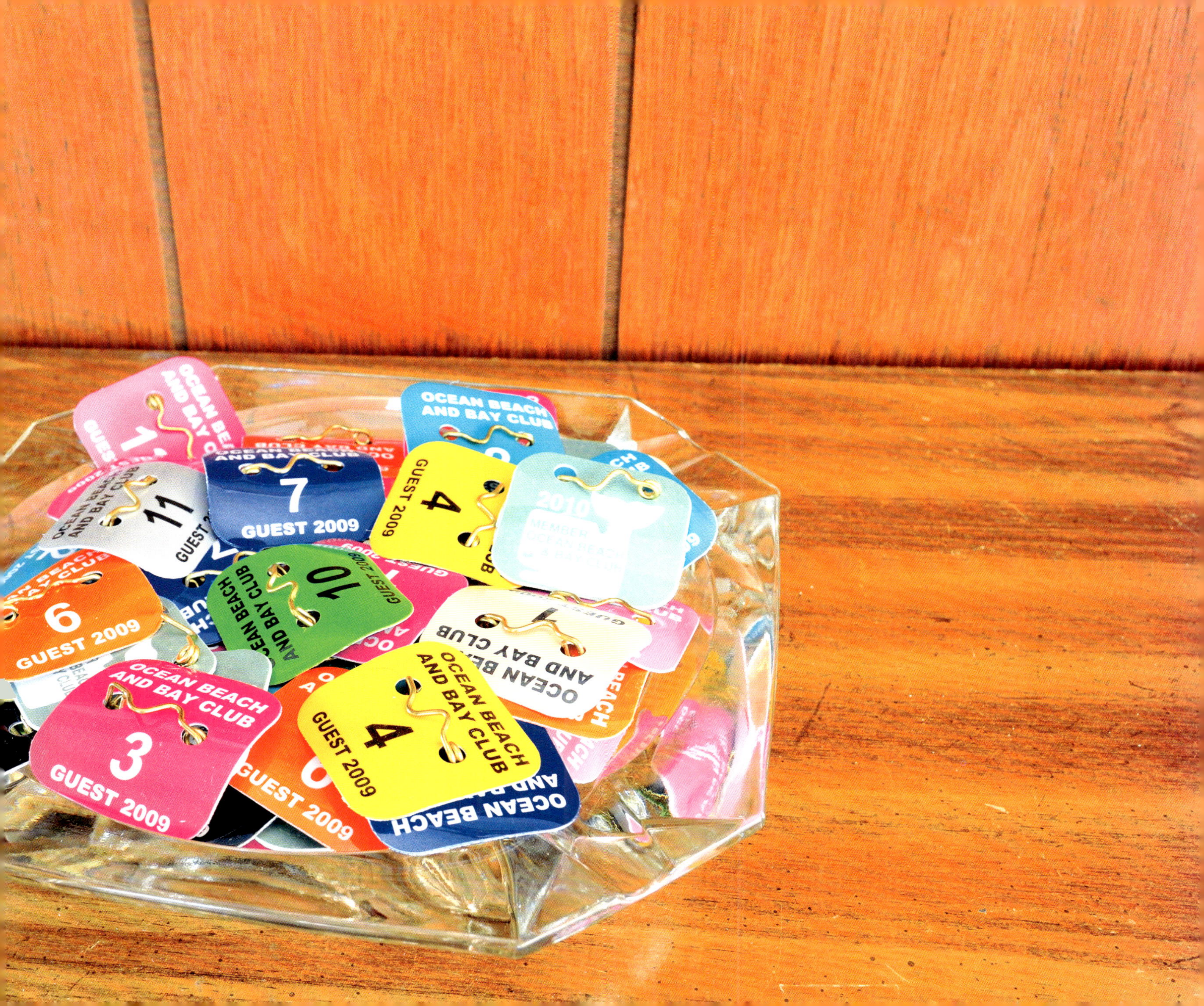
OCEAN BEACH
AND BAY CLUB
7
GUEST 2009
6
GUEST 2009
3
GUEST 2009
4
GUEST 2009
OCEAN BEACH
AND BAY CLUB
4
GUEST 2009
10
OCEAN BEACH
AND BAY CLUB
11
OCEAN BEACH
AND BAY CLUB
OCEAN BEACH

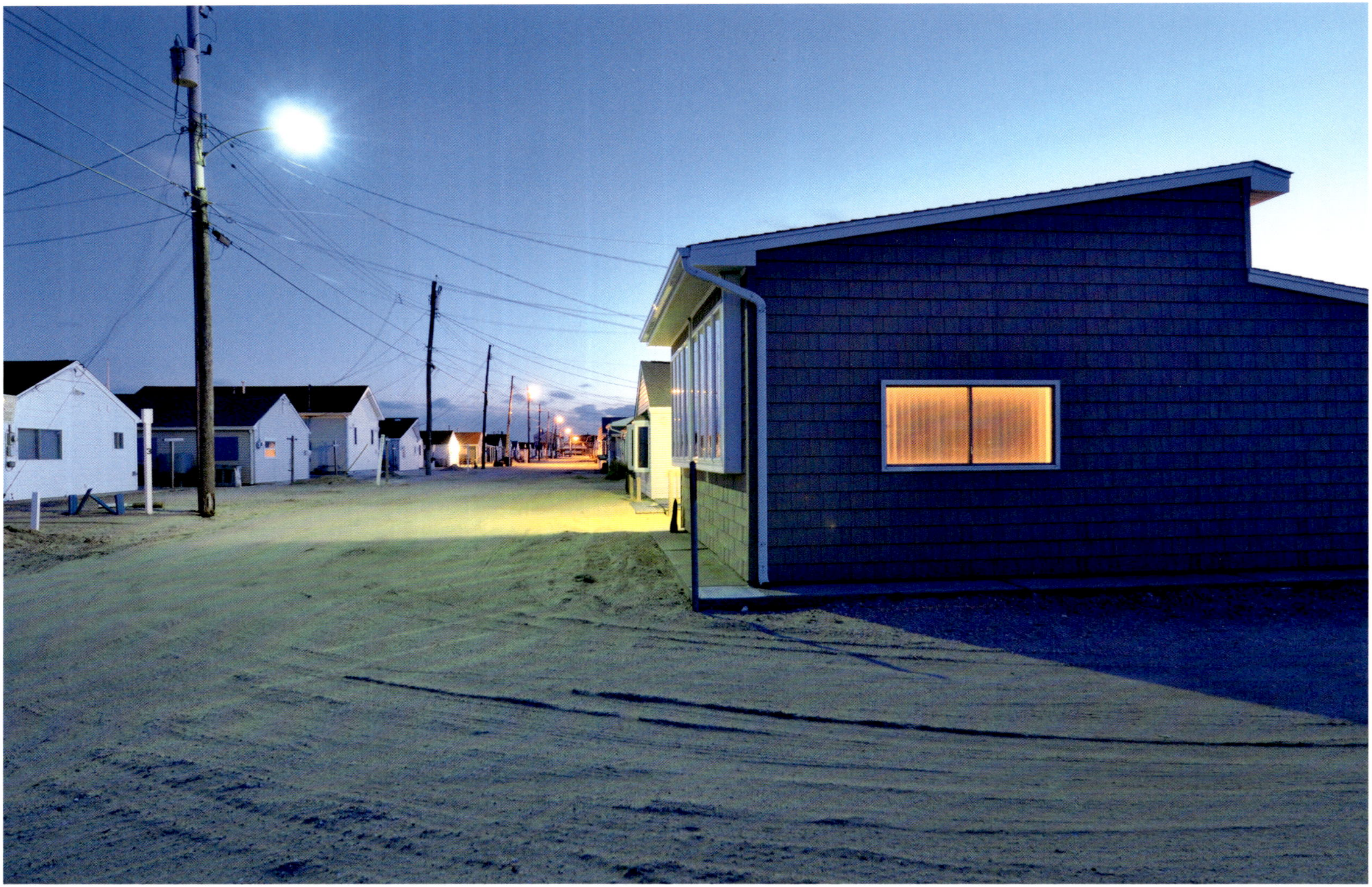

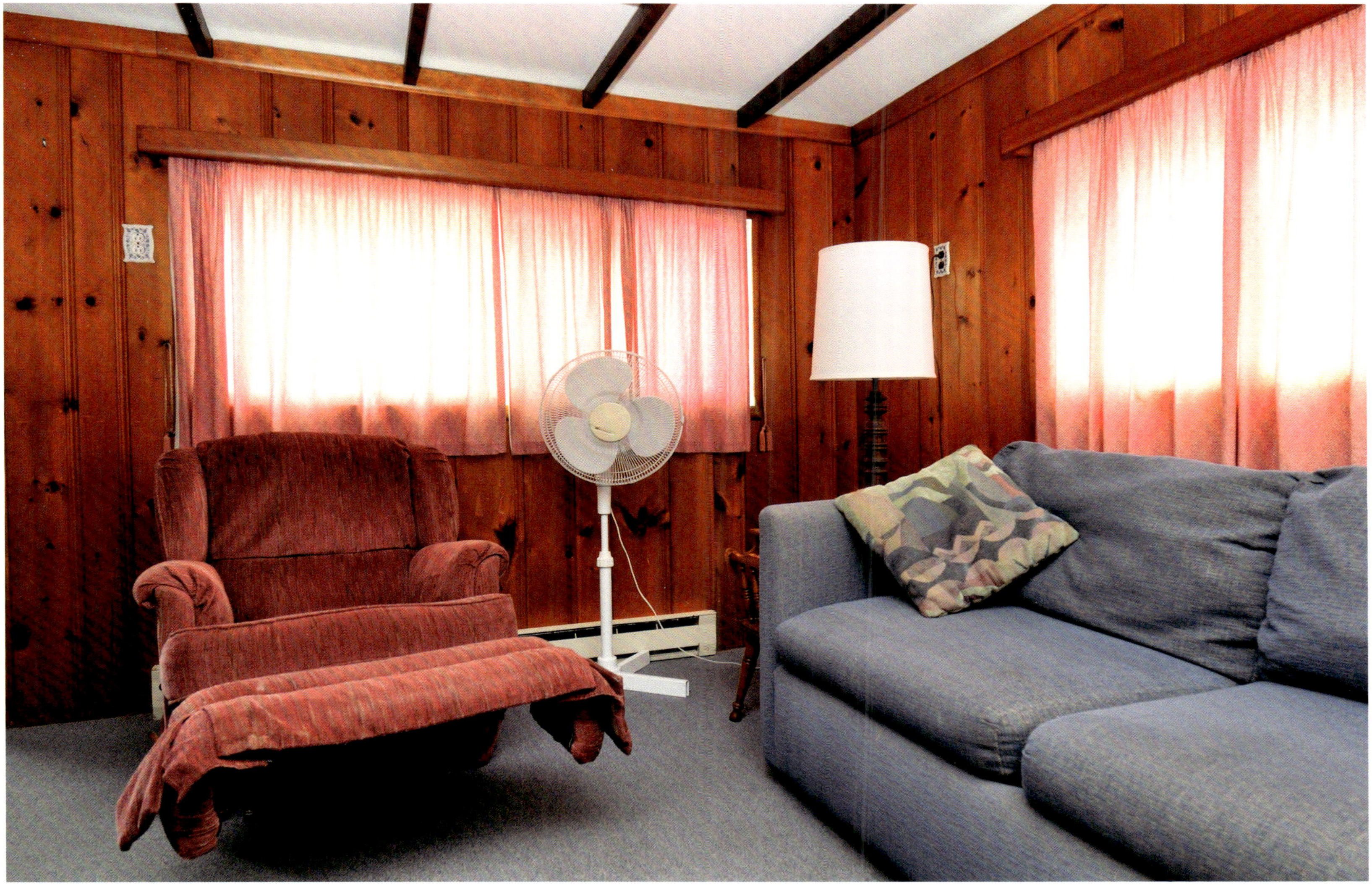

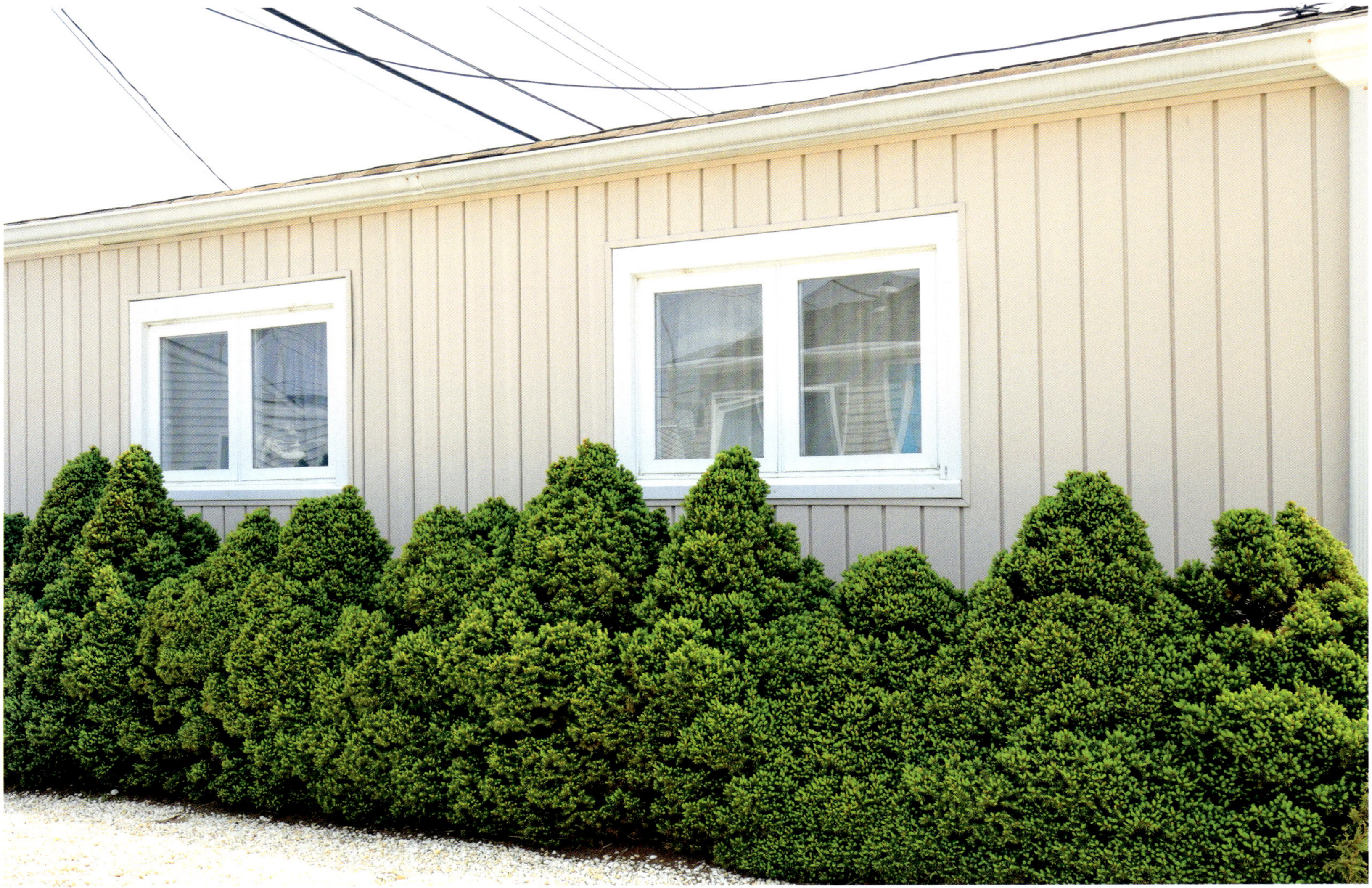

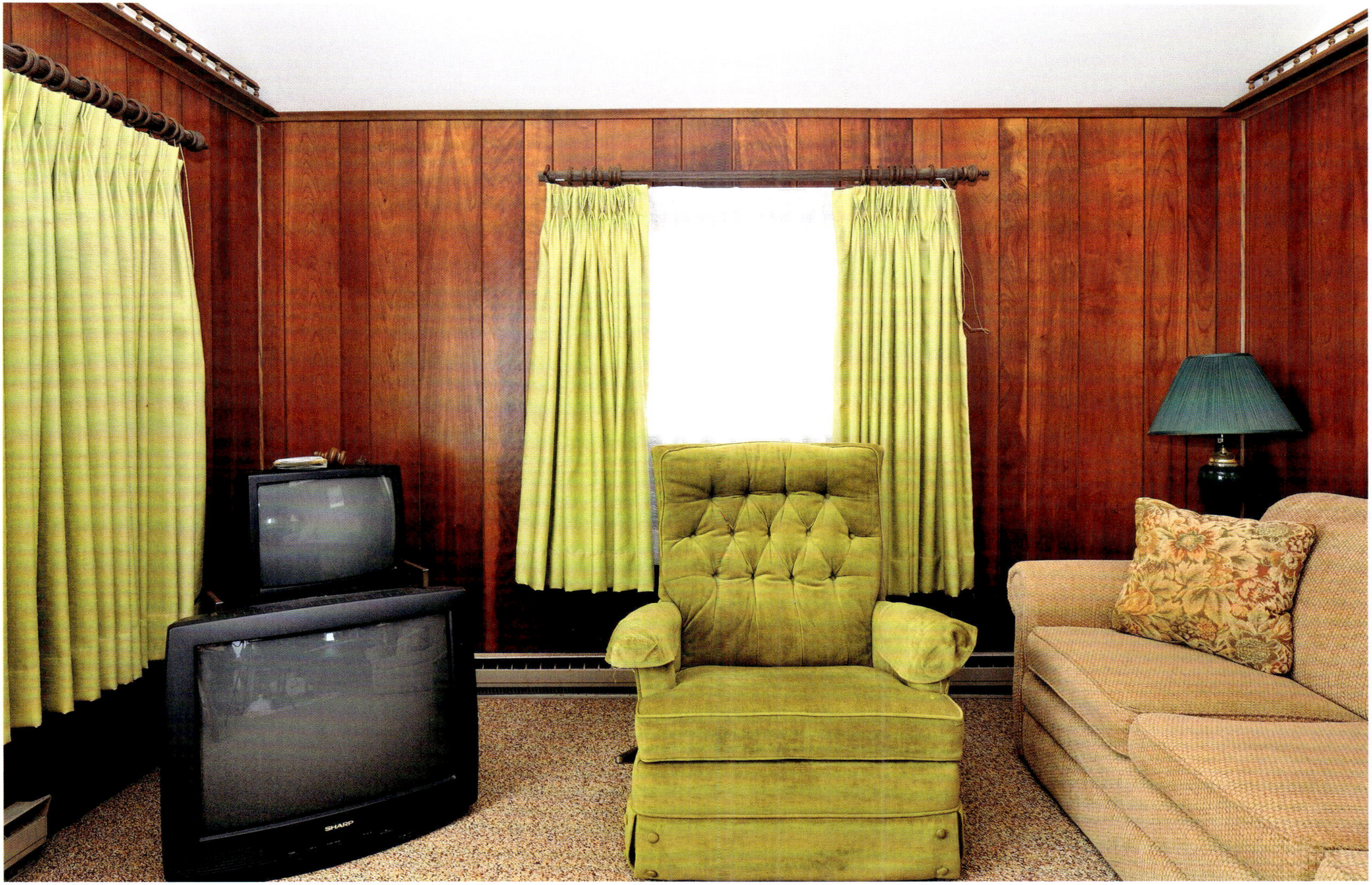
SHARP

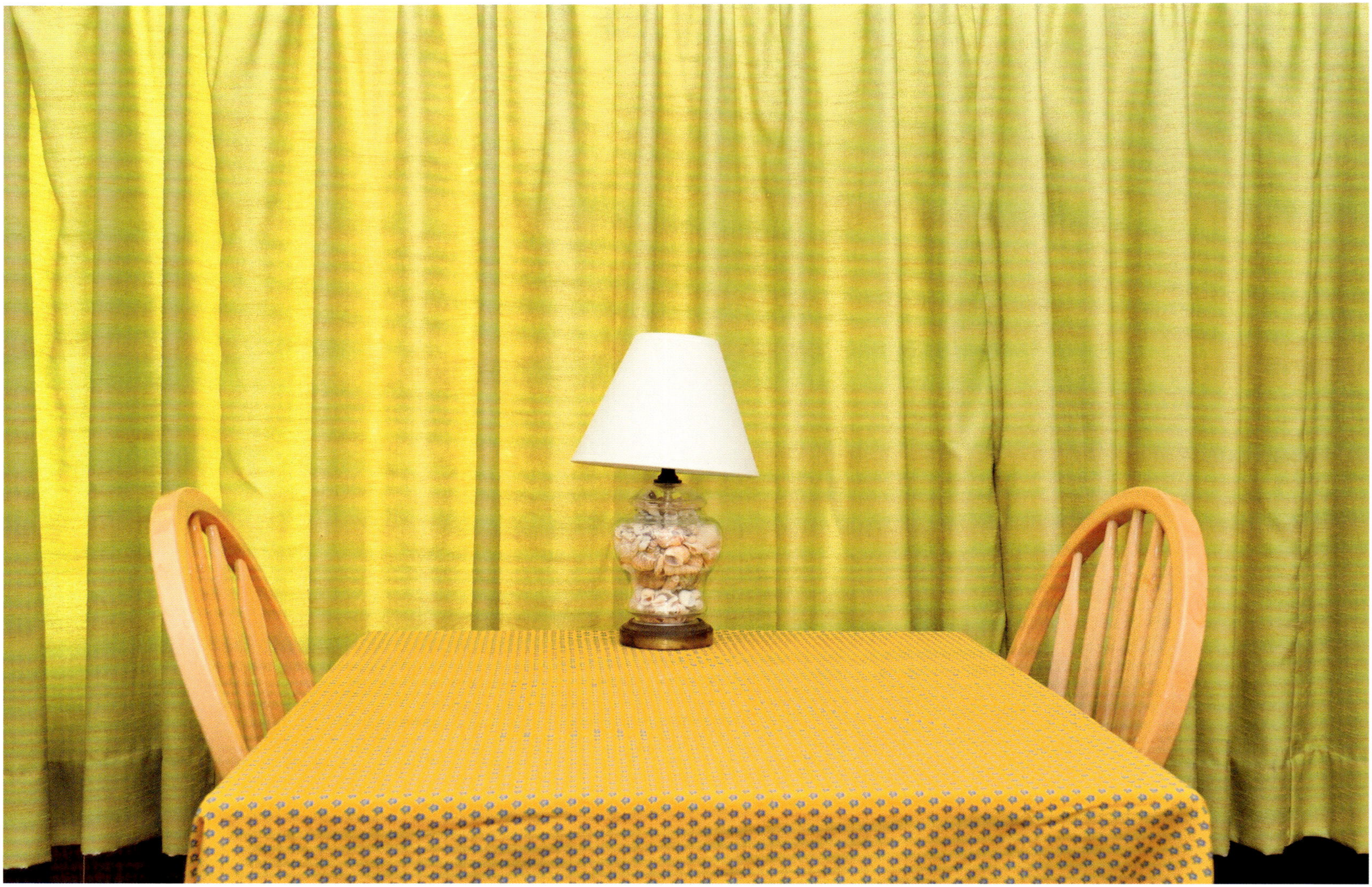

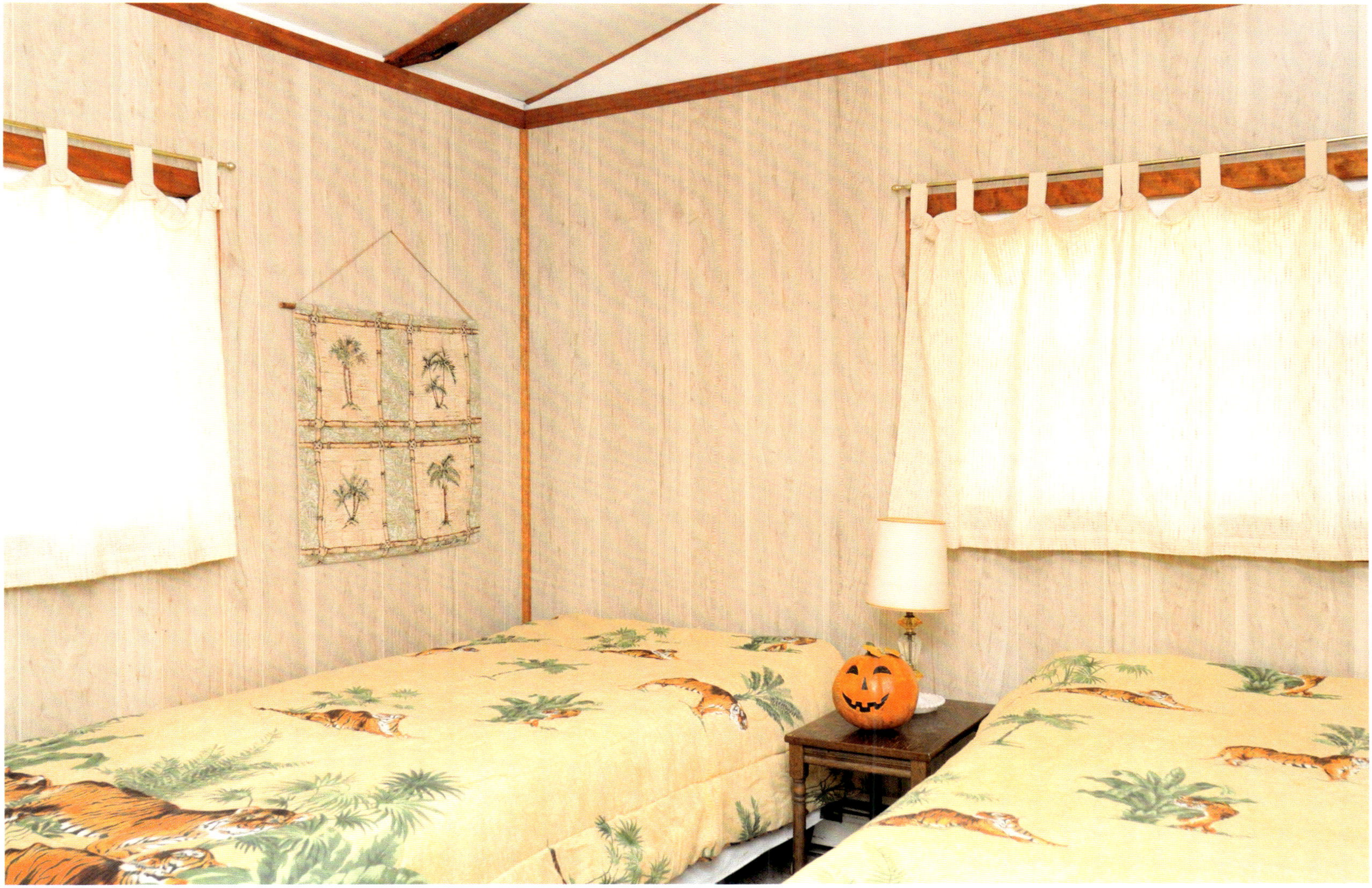

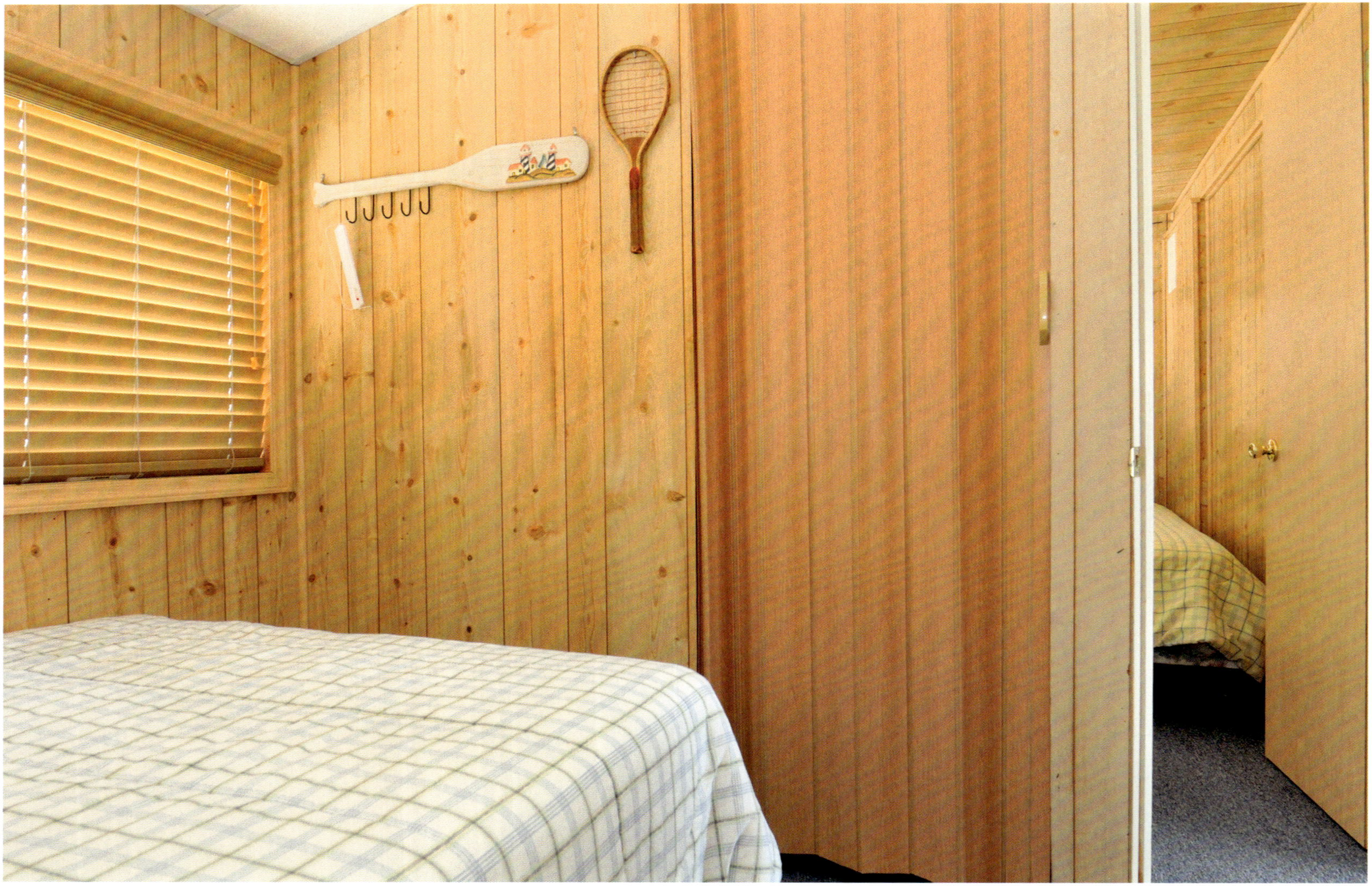

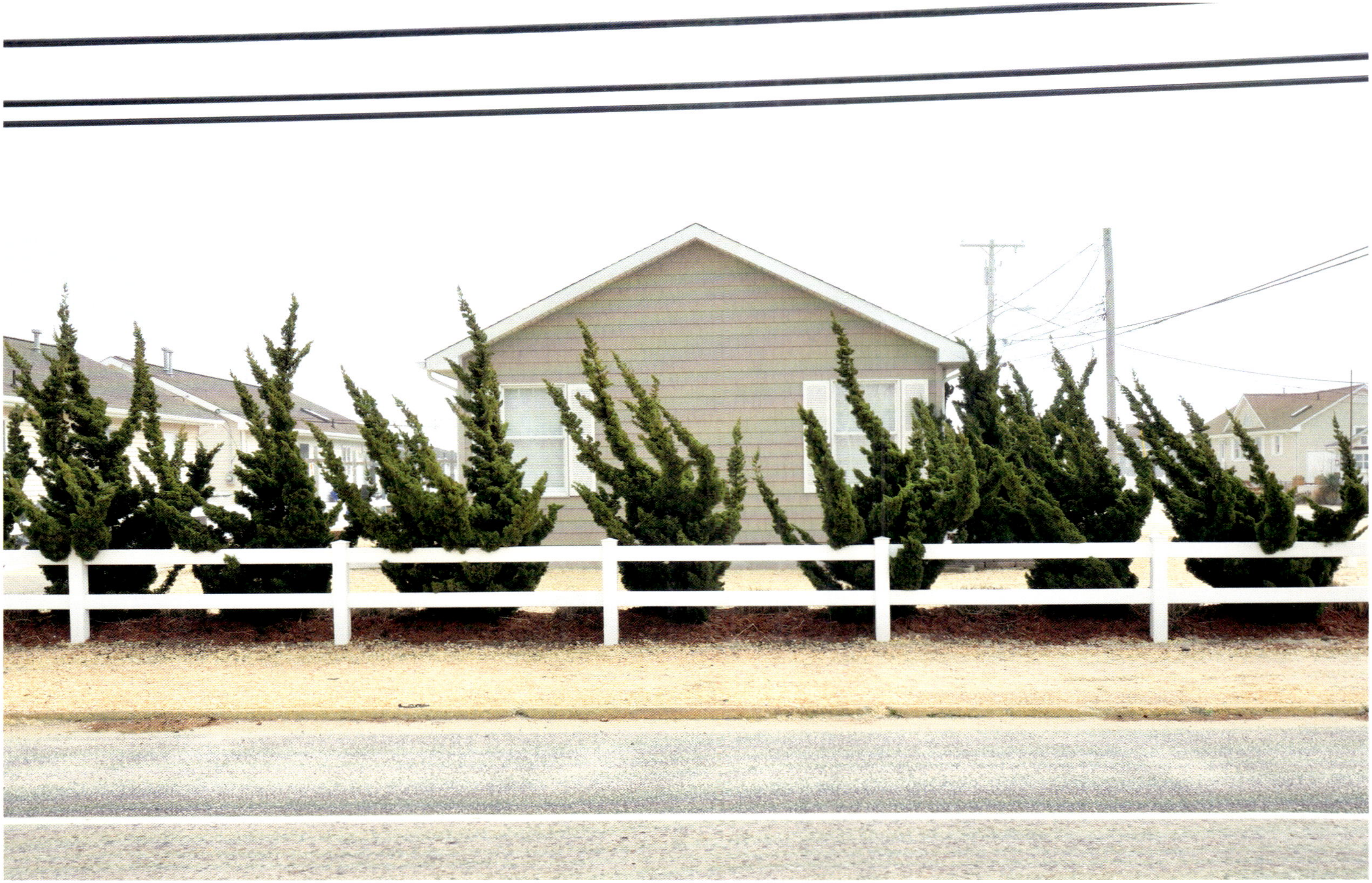

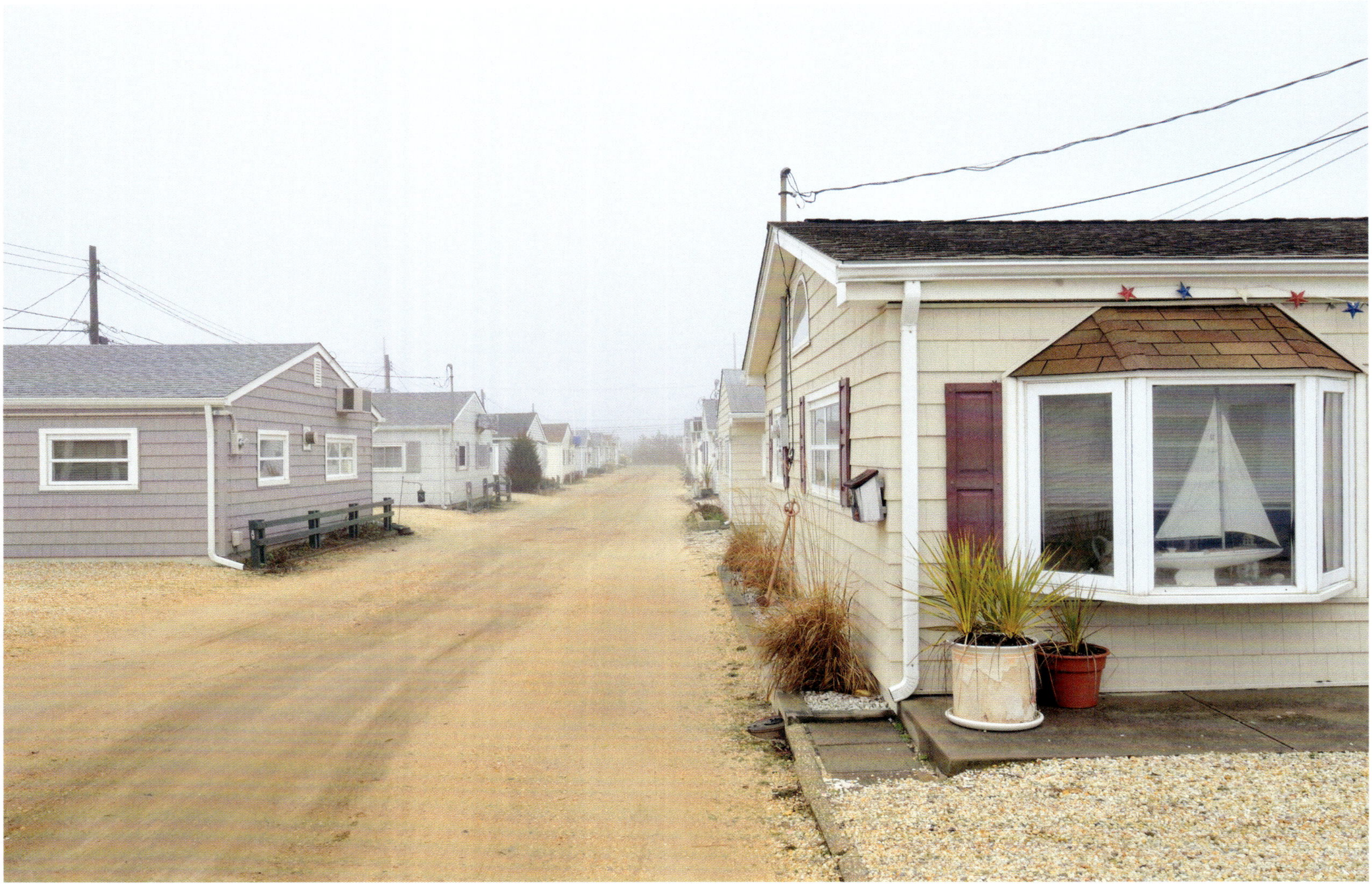

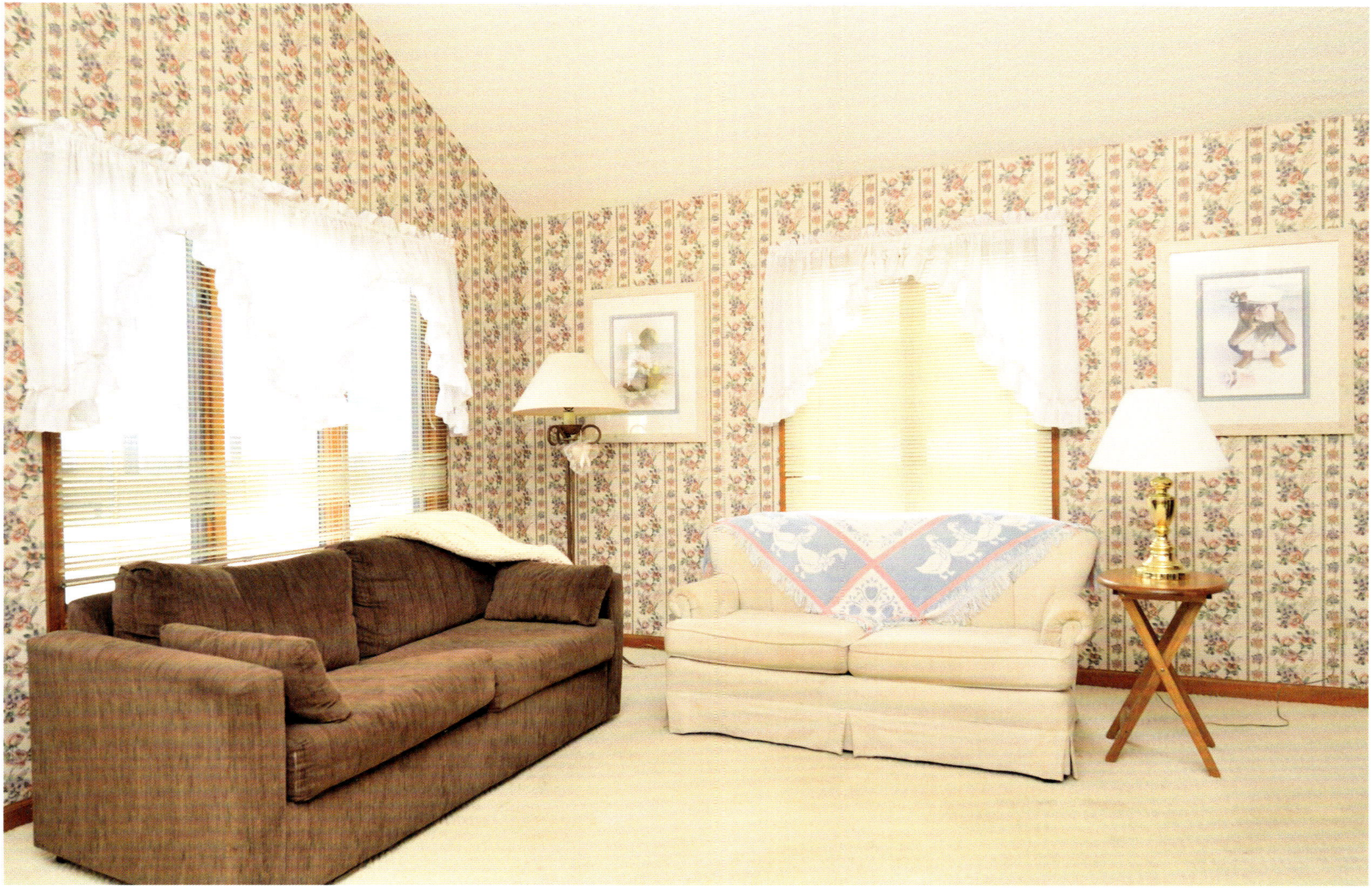

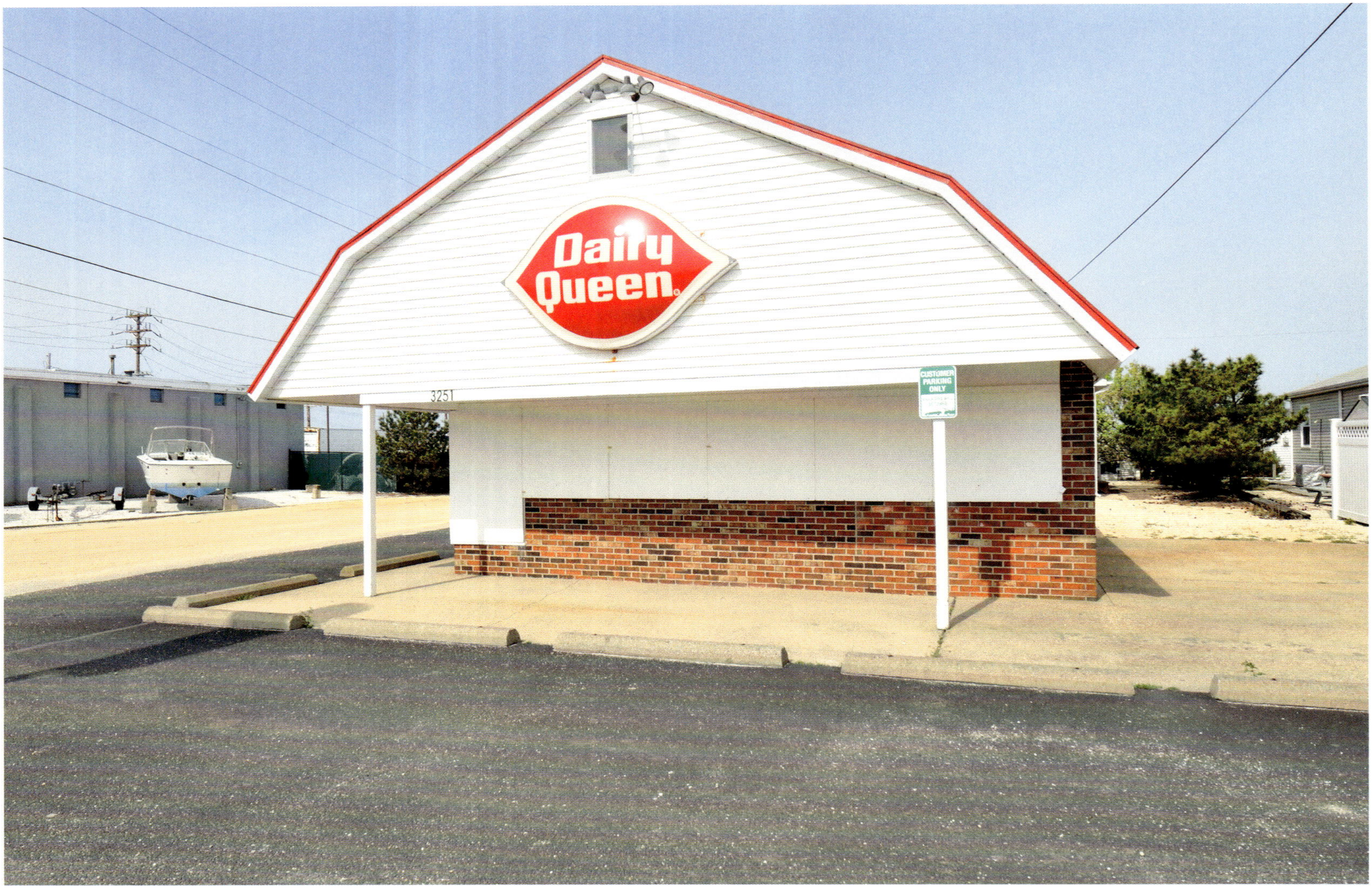
Dairy Queen
3251
CUSTOMER PARKING ONLY

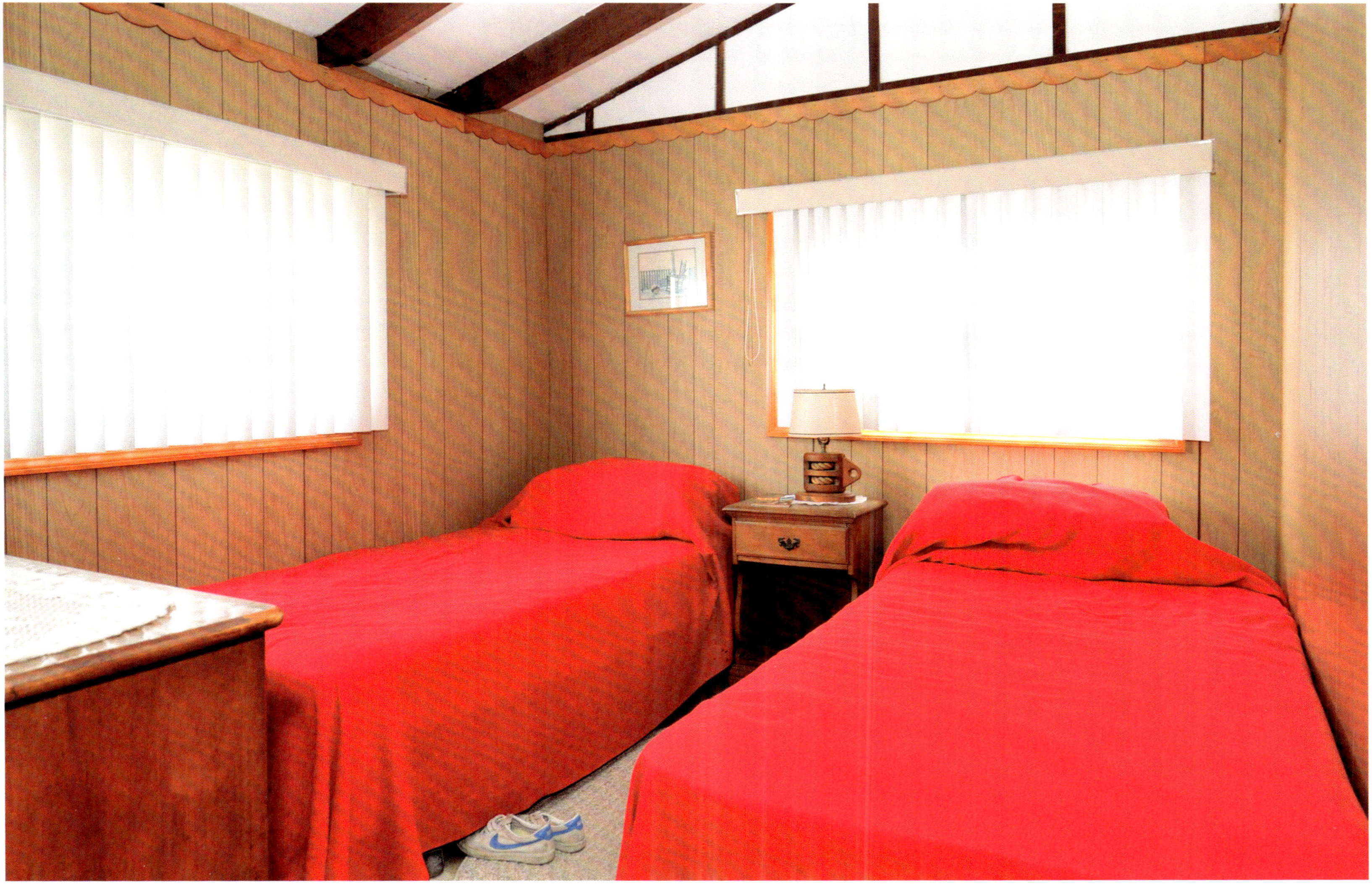

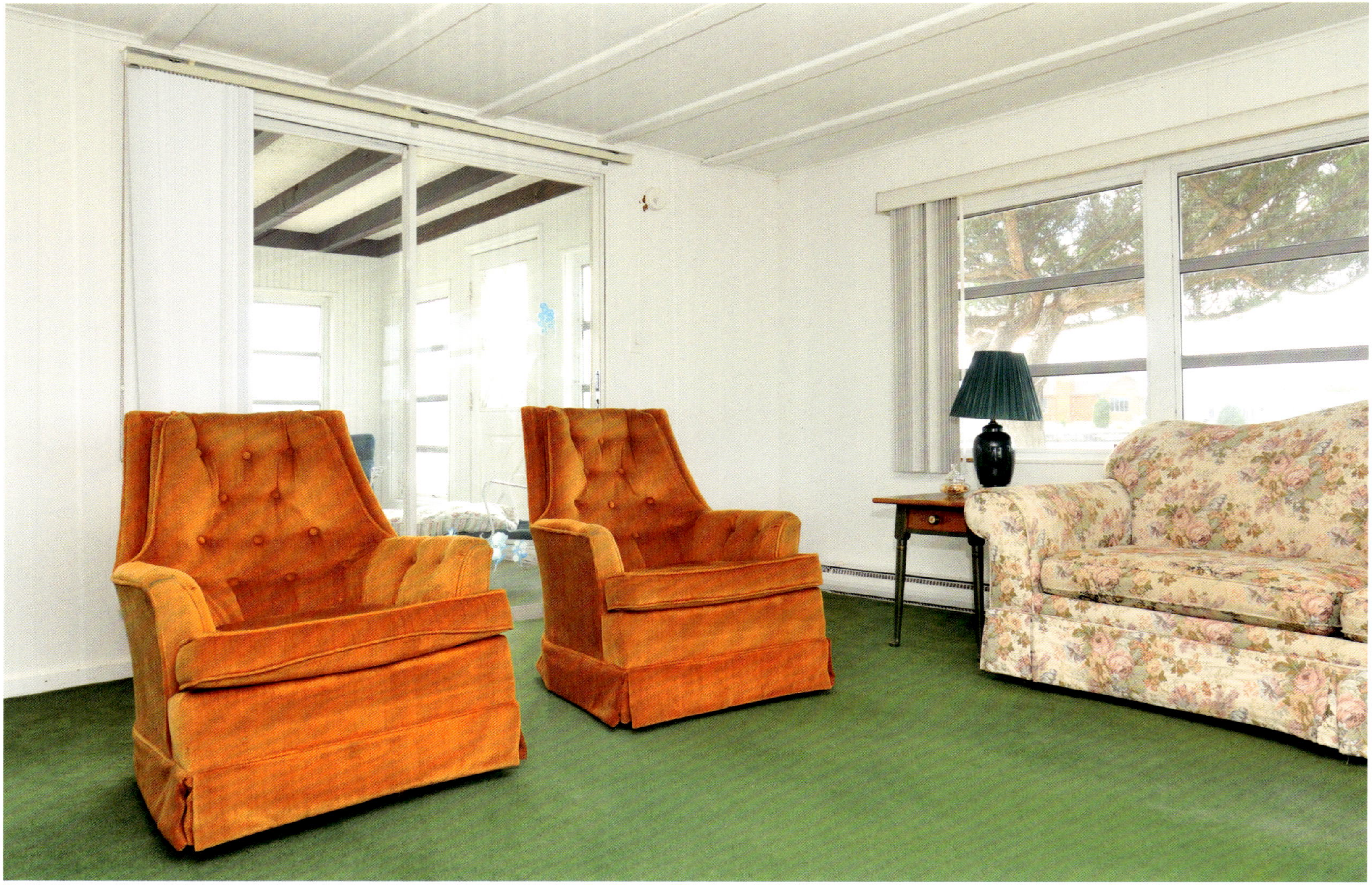

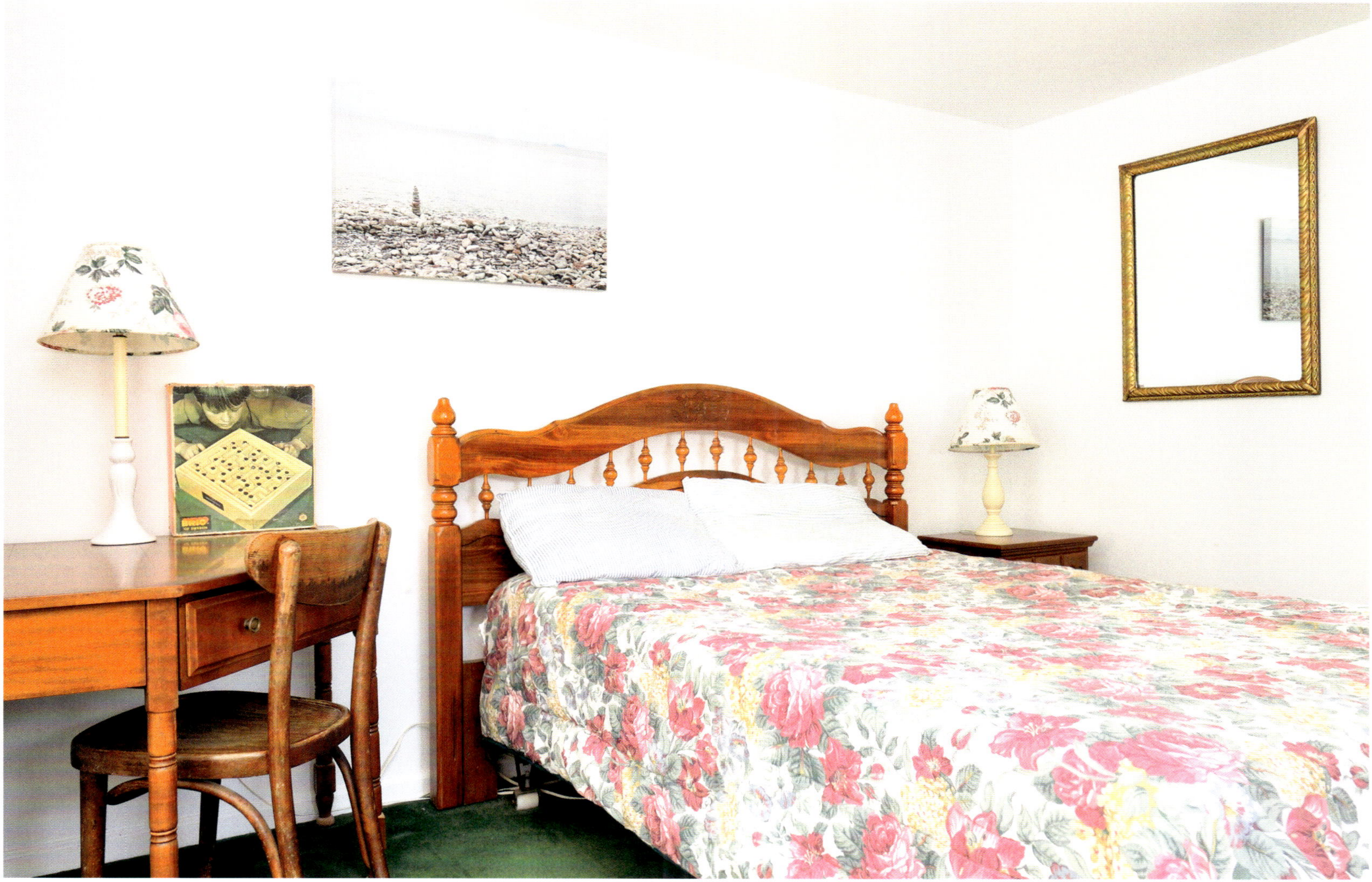

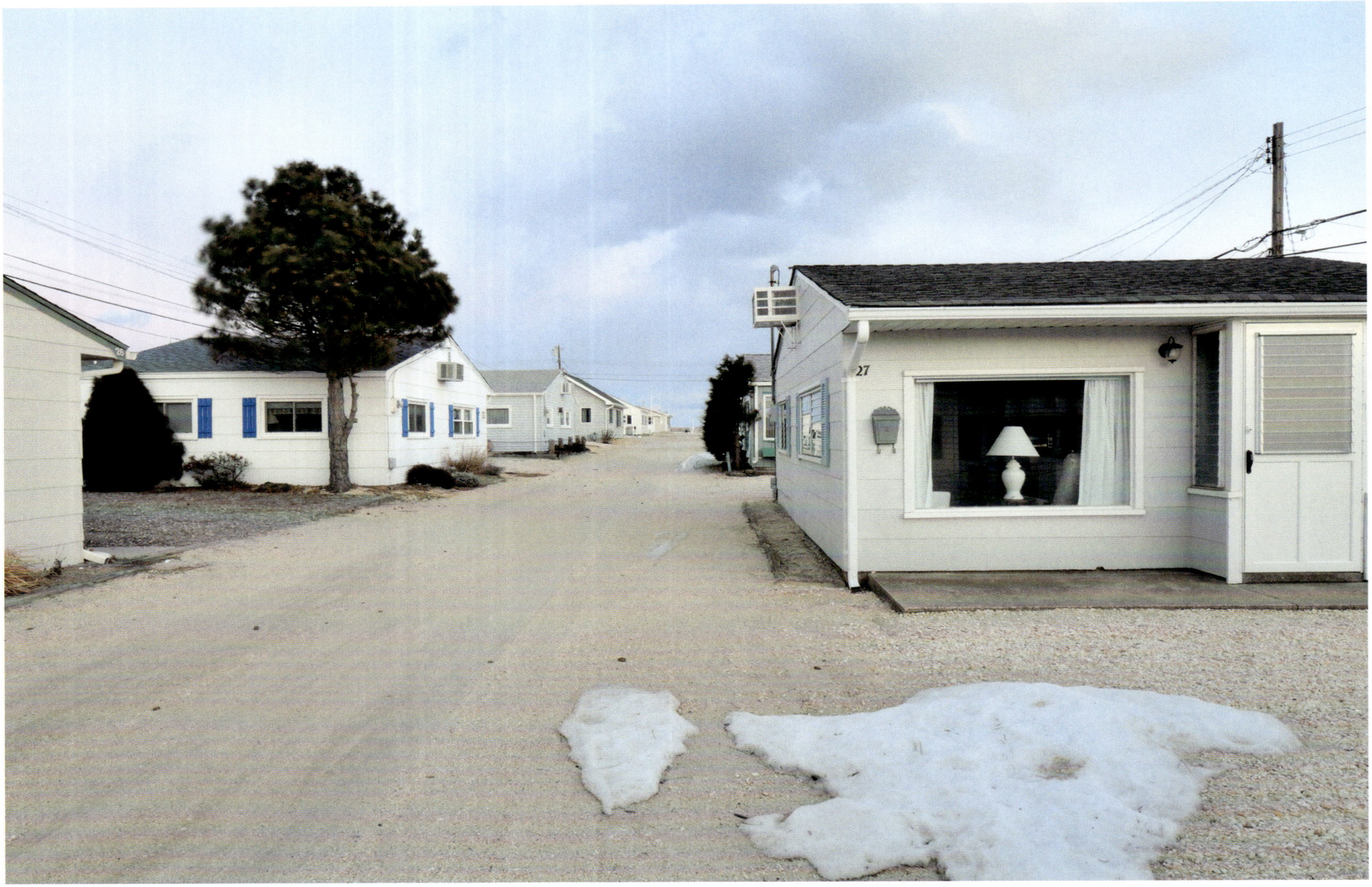

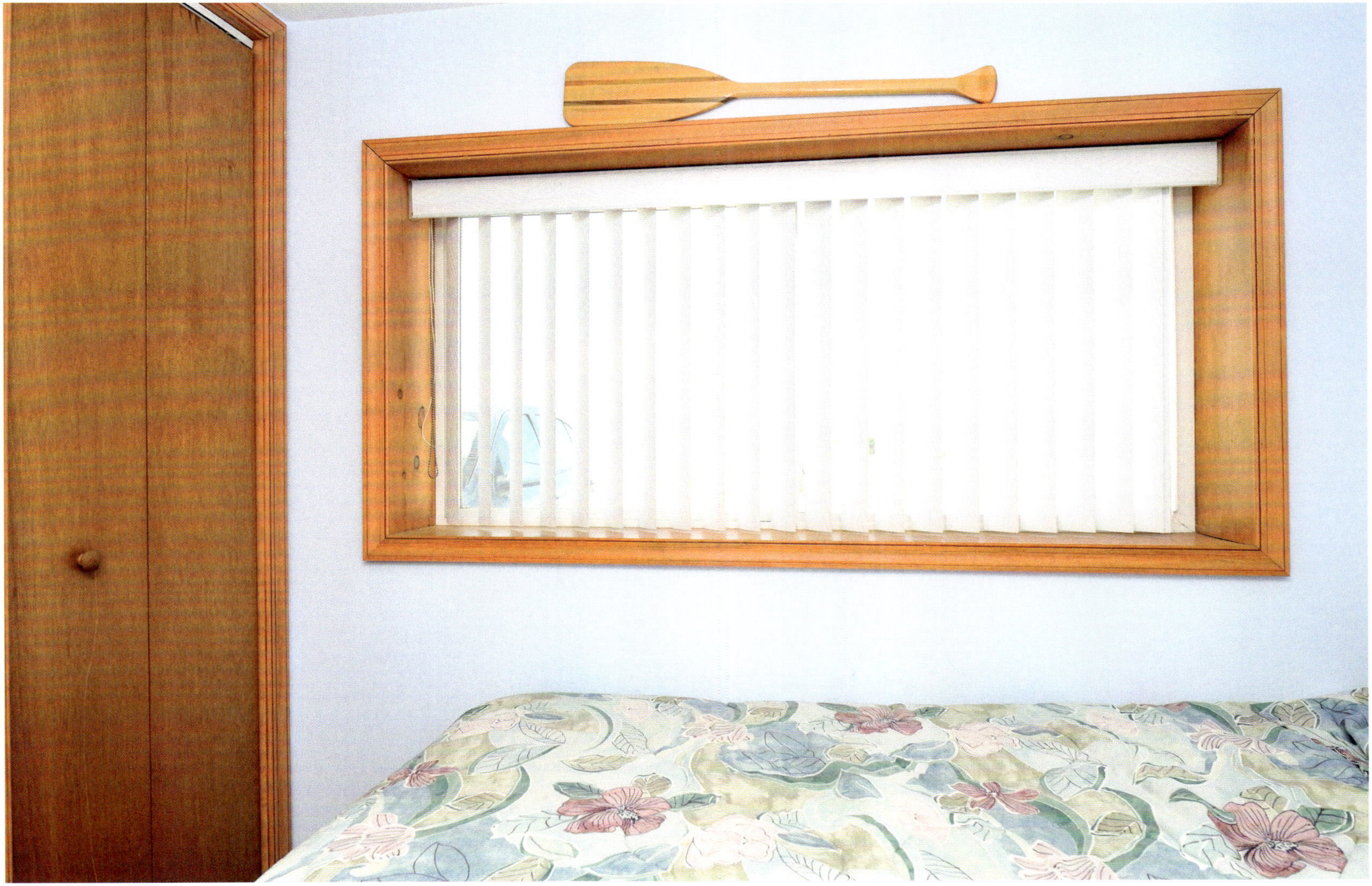

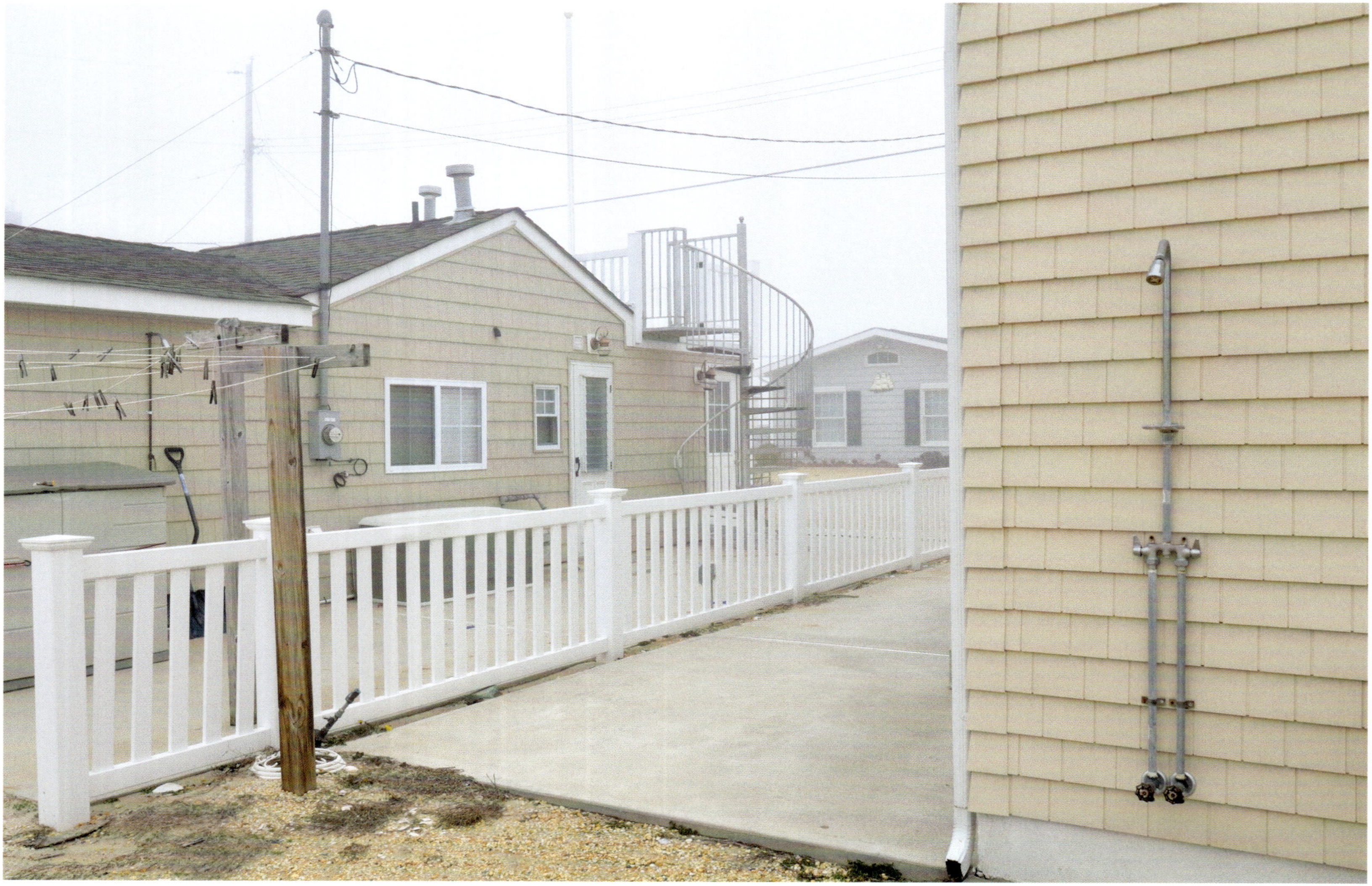

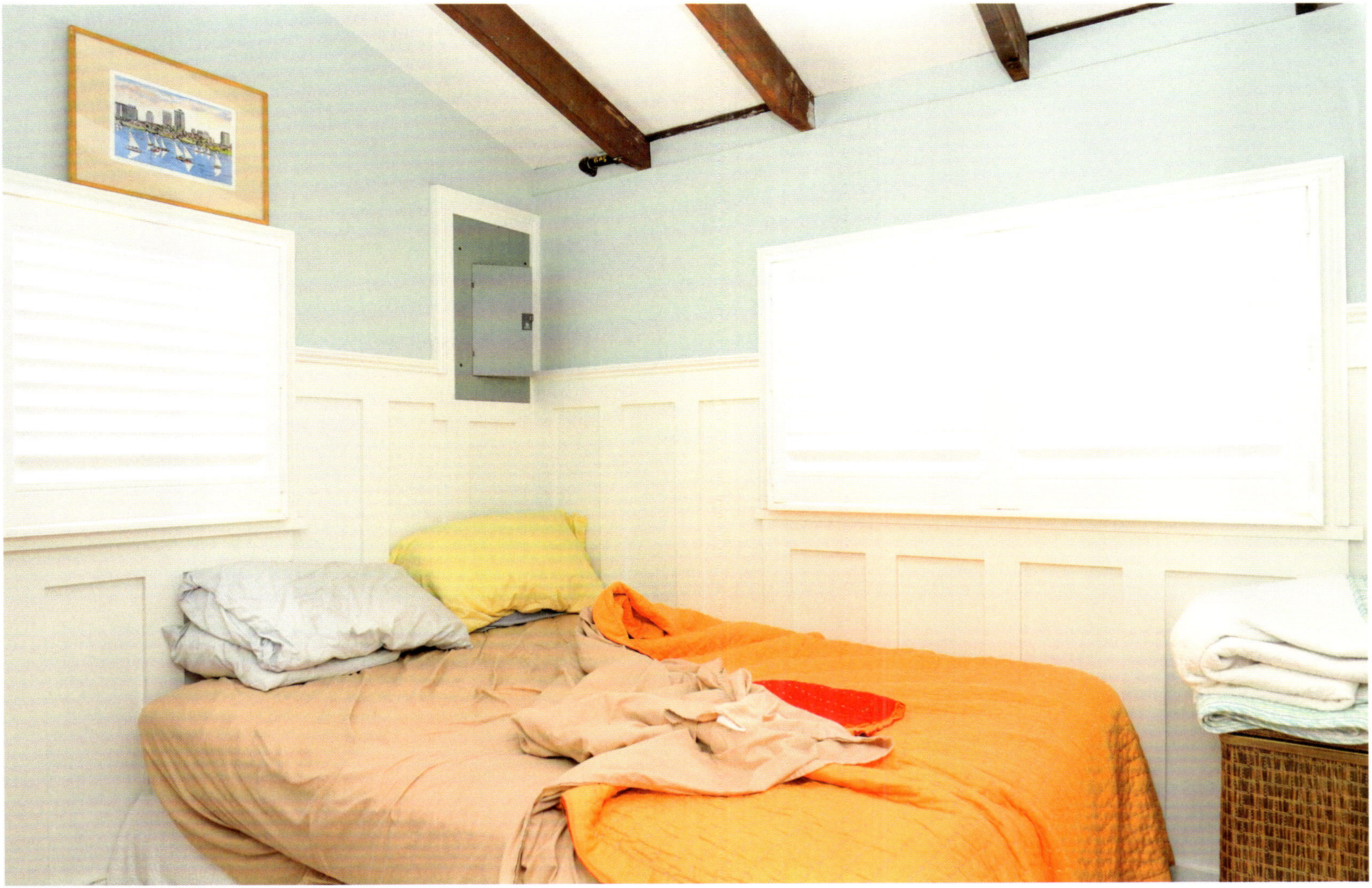

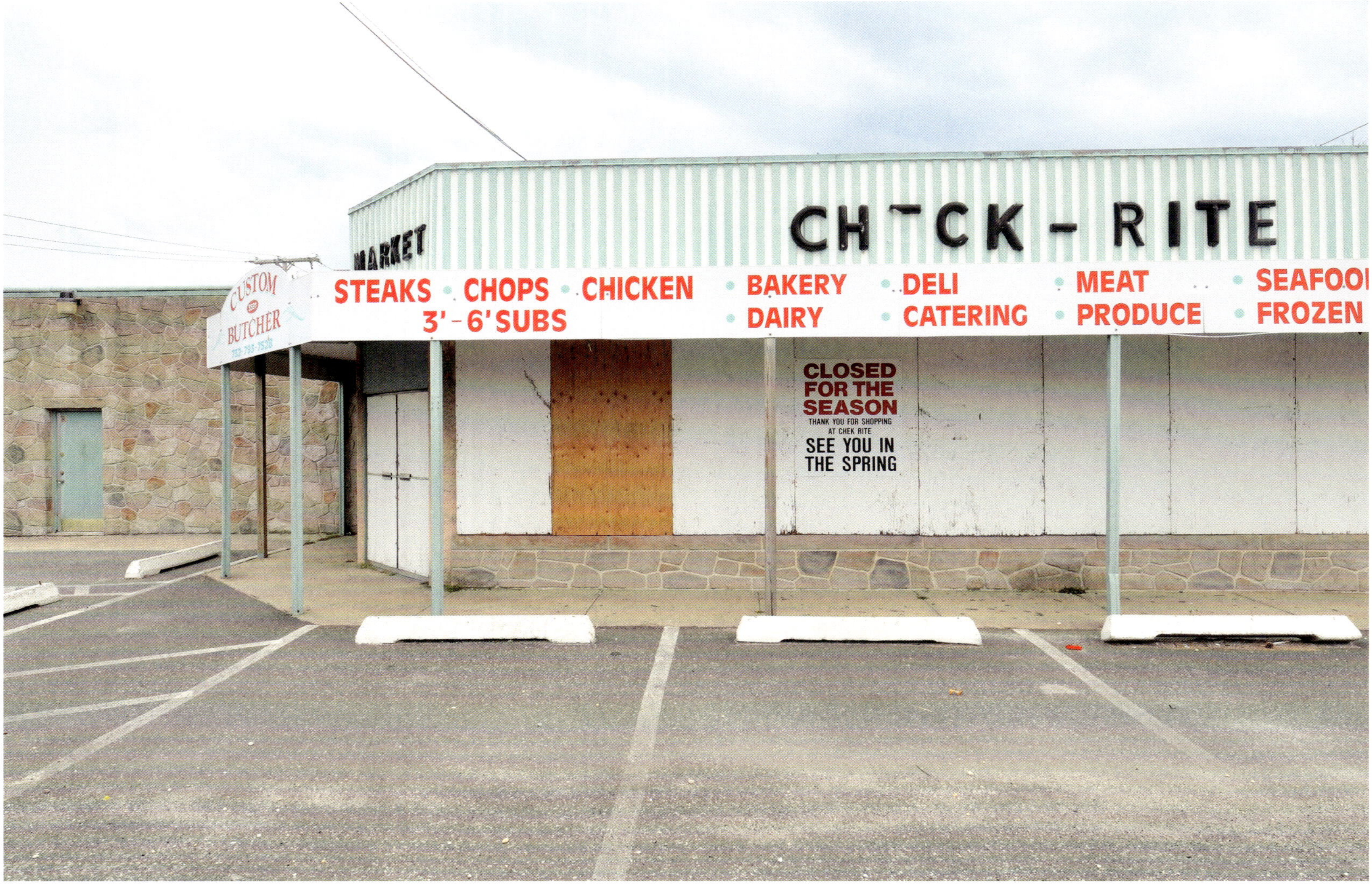
MARKET
CH CK - RITE
CUSTOM
BUTCHER
STEAKS · CHOPS · CHICKEN
3'-6' SUBS
BAKERY
DAIRY
DELI
CATERING
MEAT
PRODUCE
FROZEN
CLOSED FOR THE SEASON
THANK YOU FOR SHOPPING AT CHEK RITE
SEE YOU IN THE SPRING

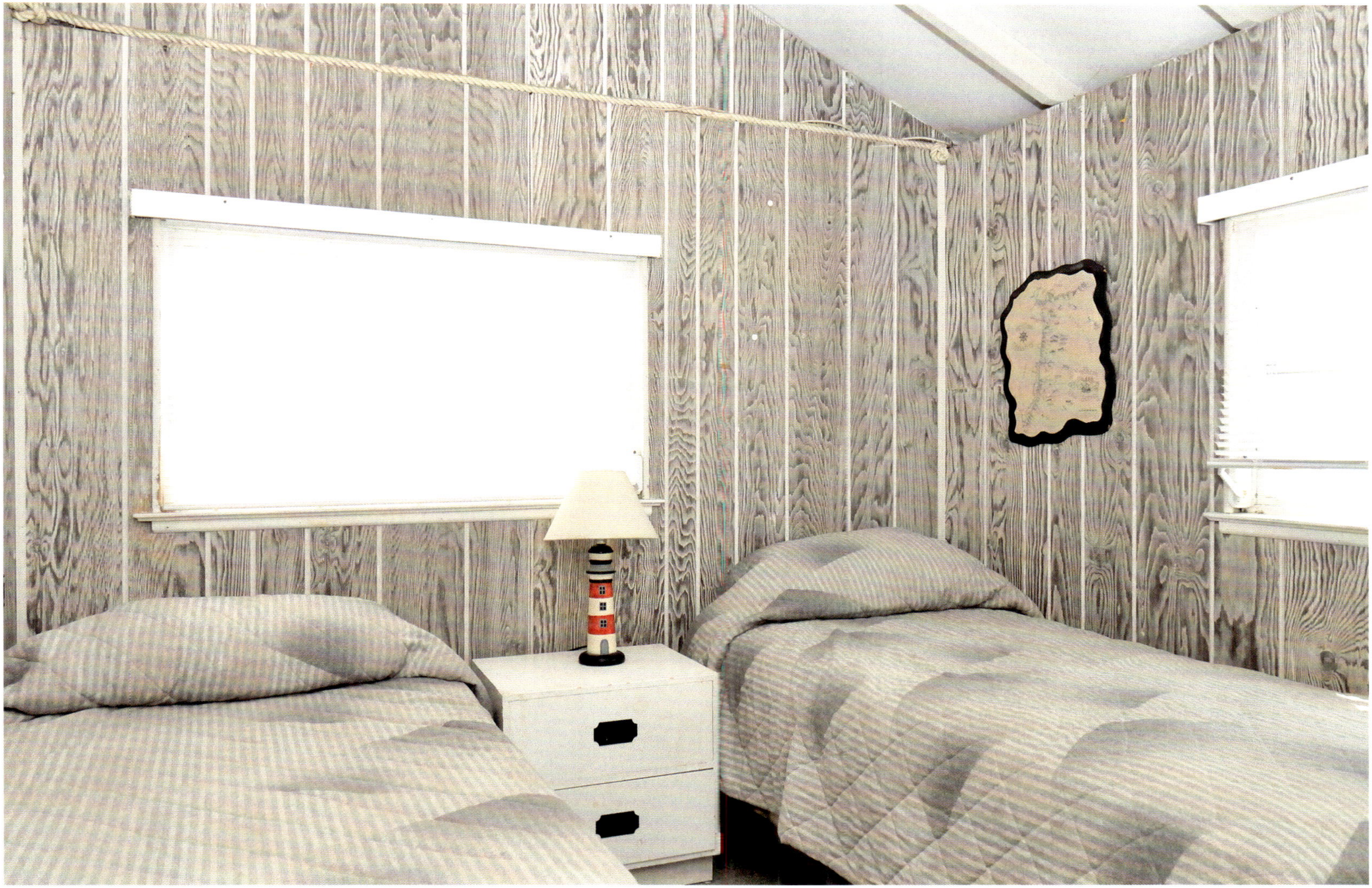

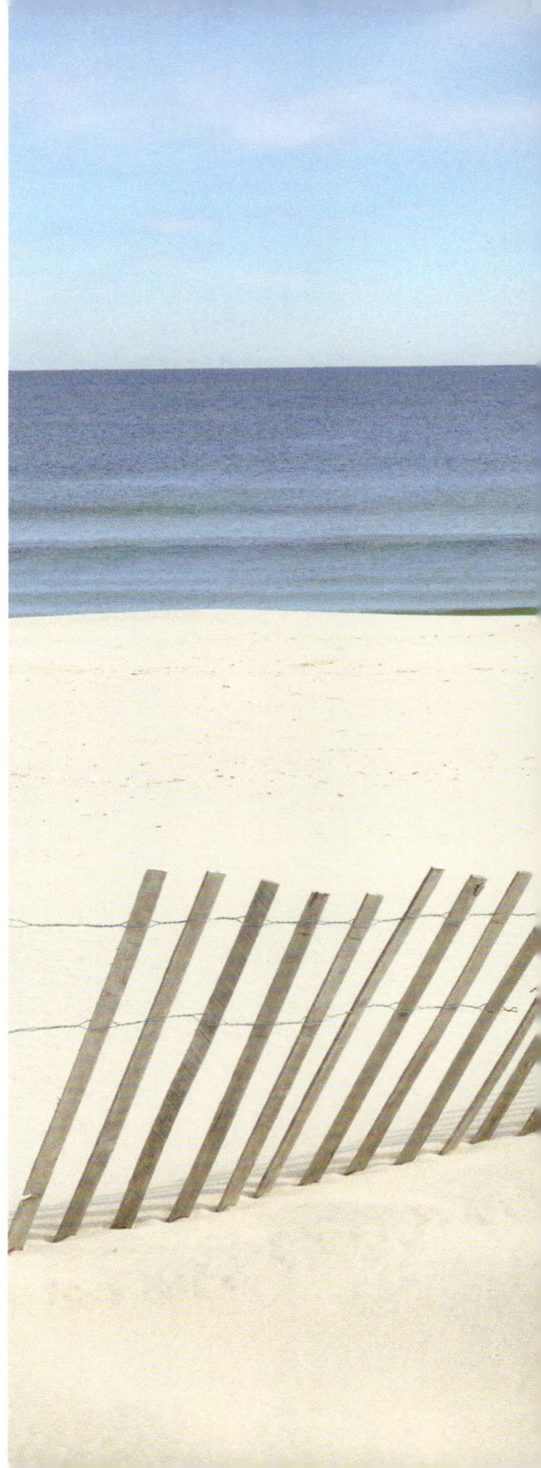

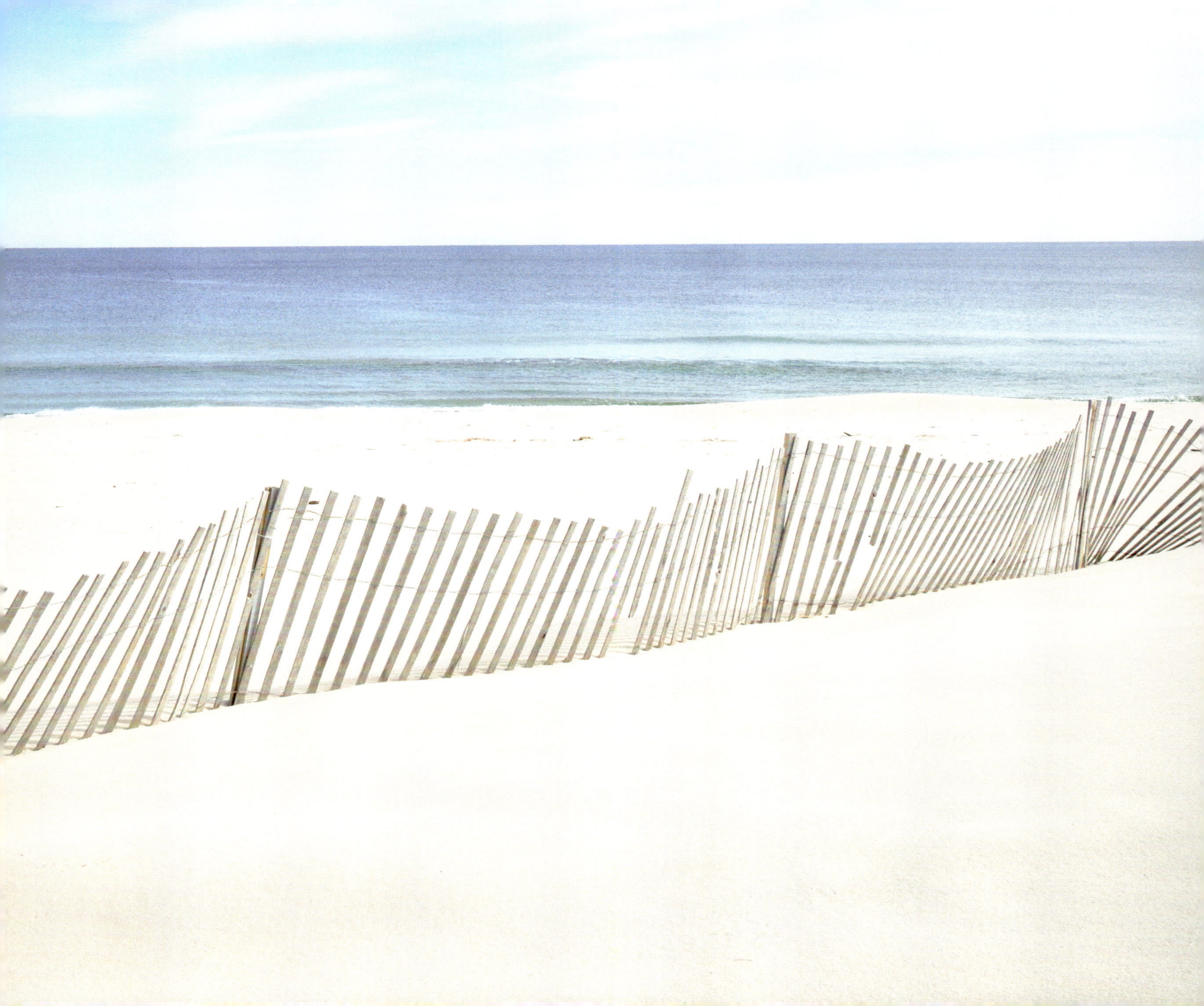

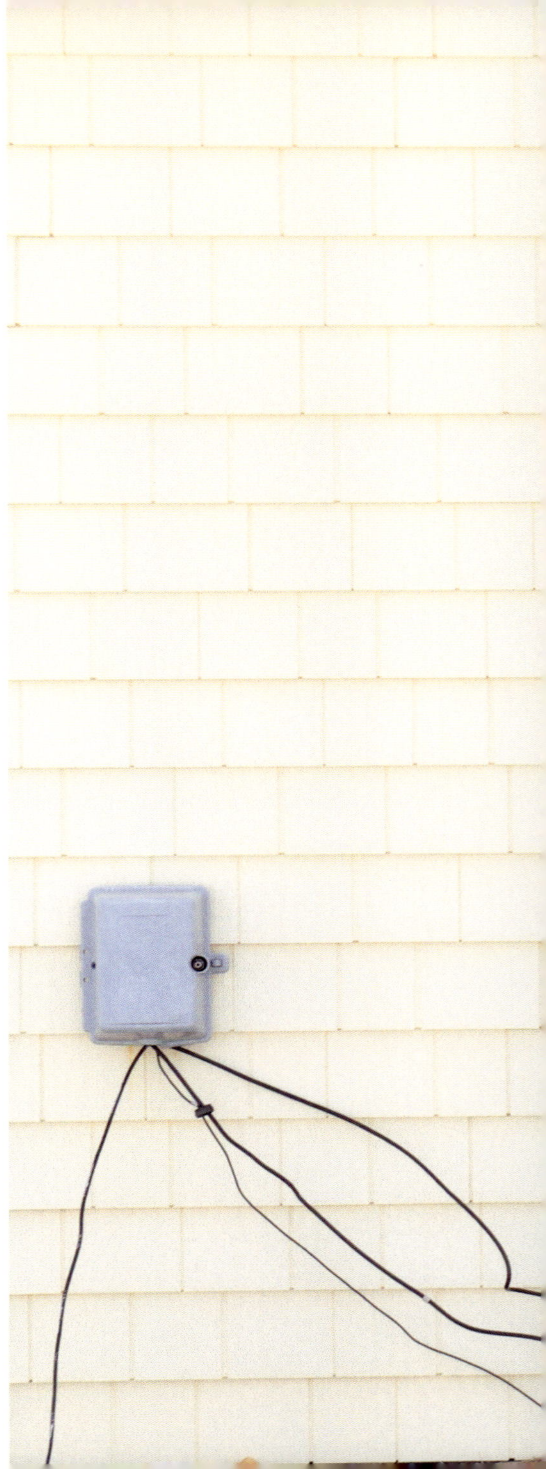

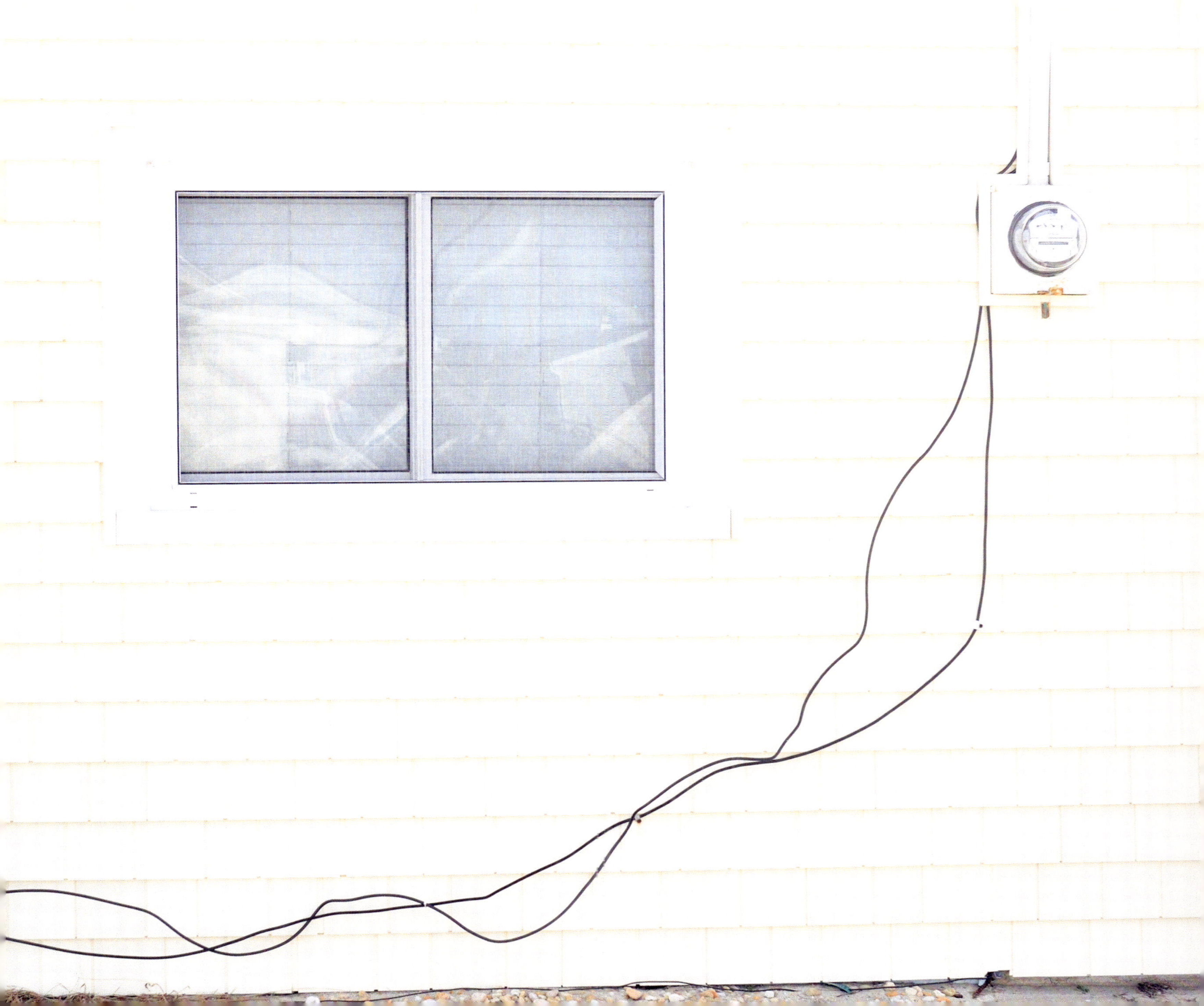

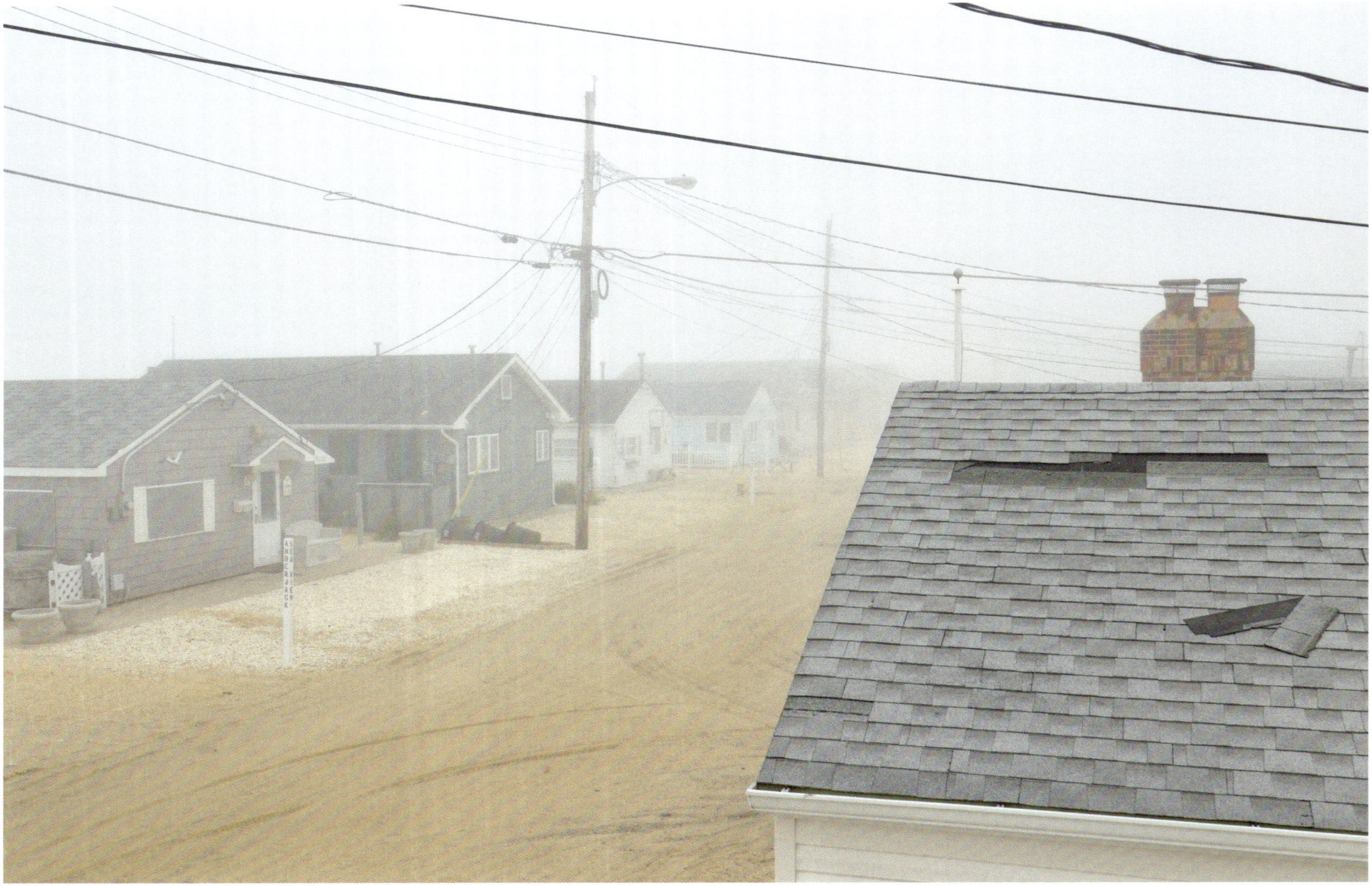

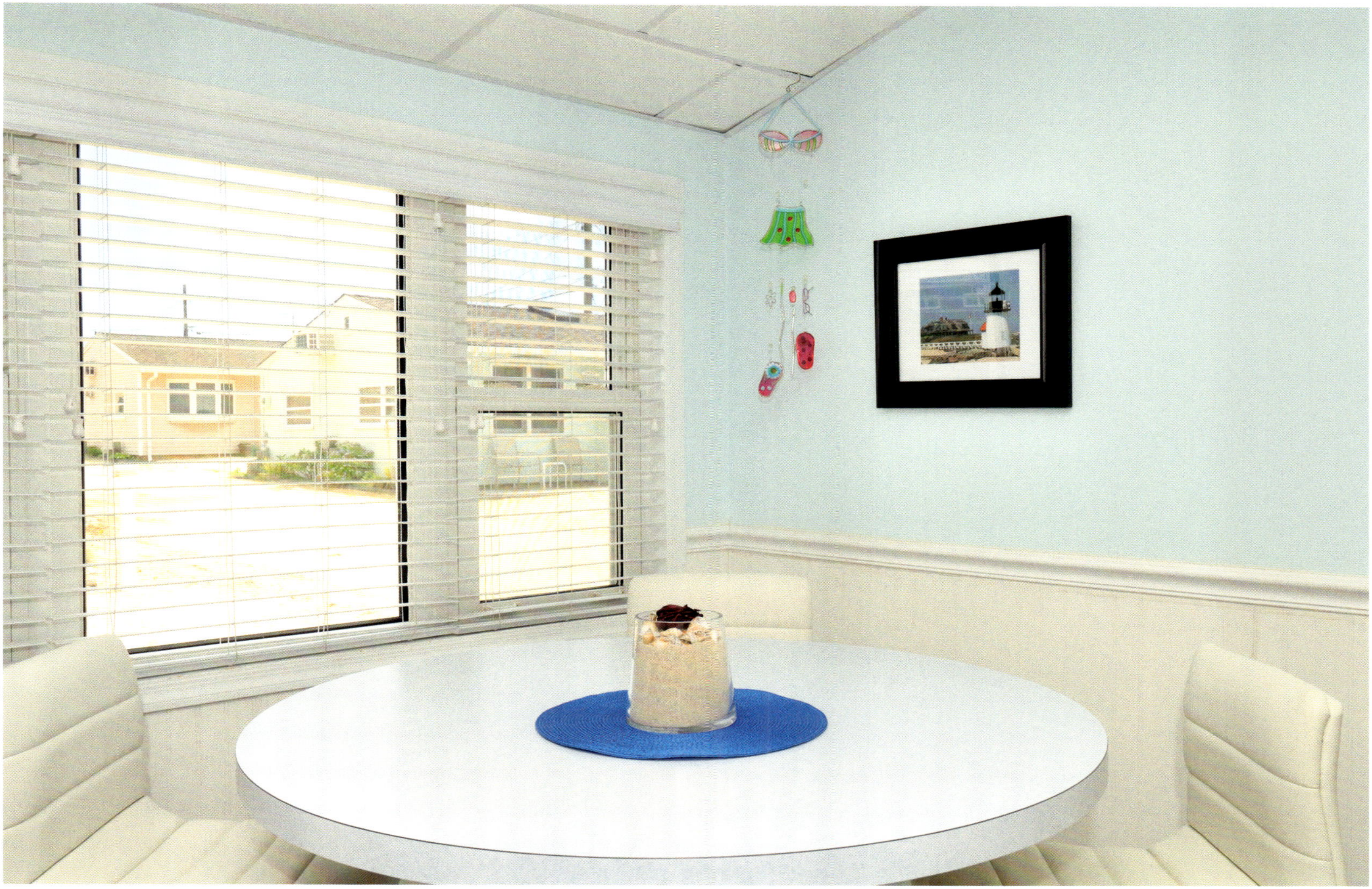

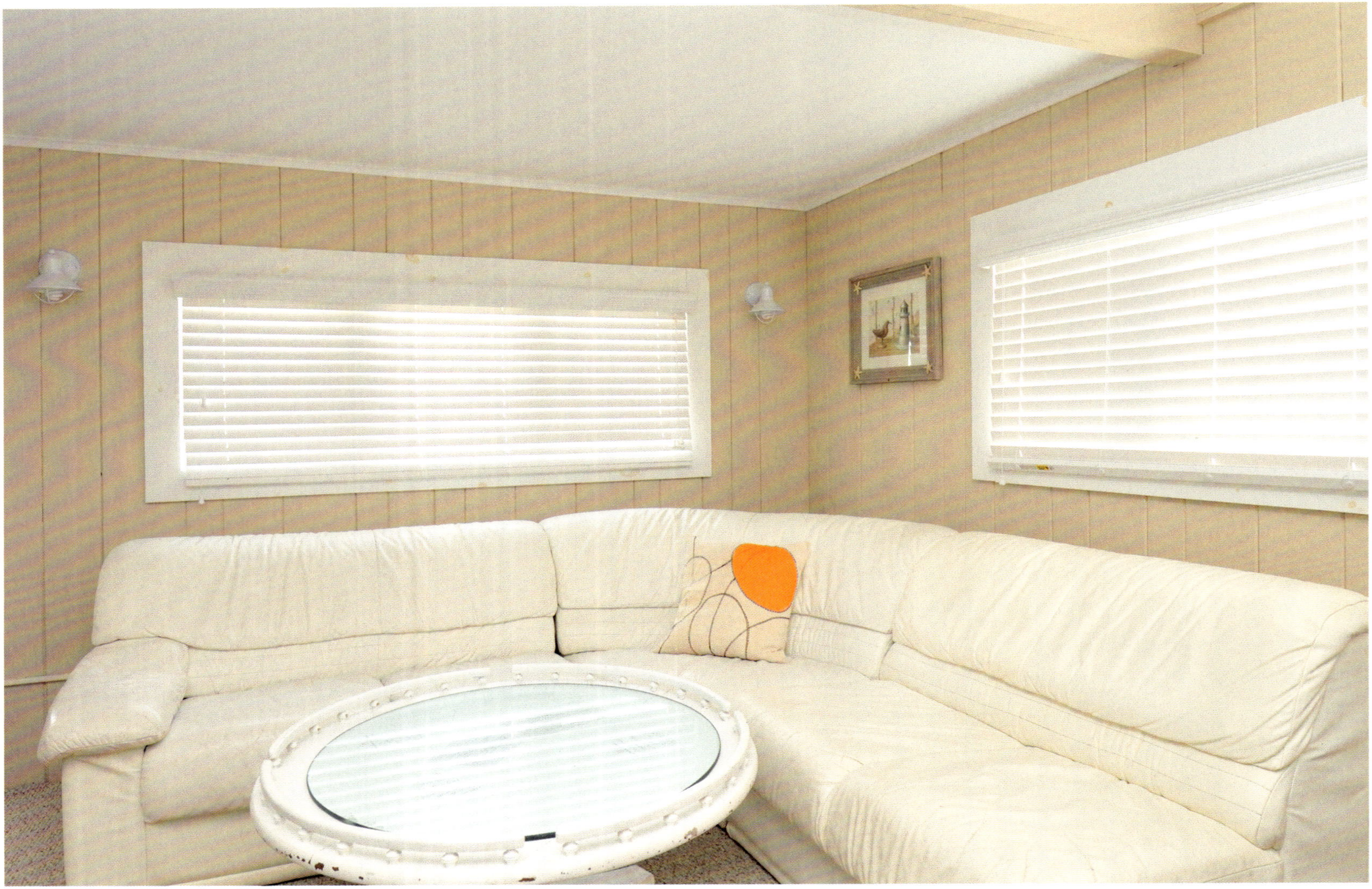

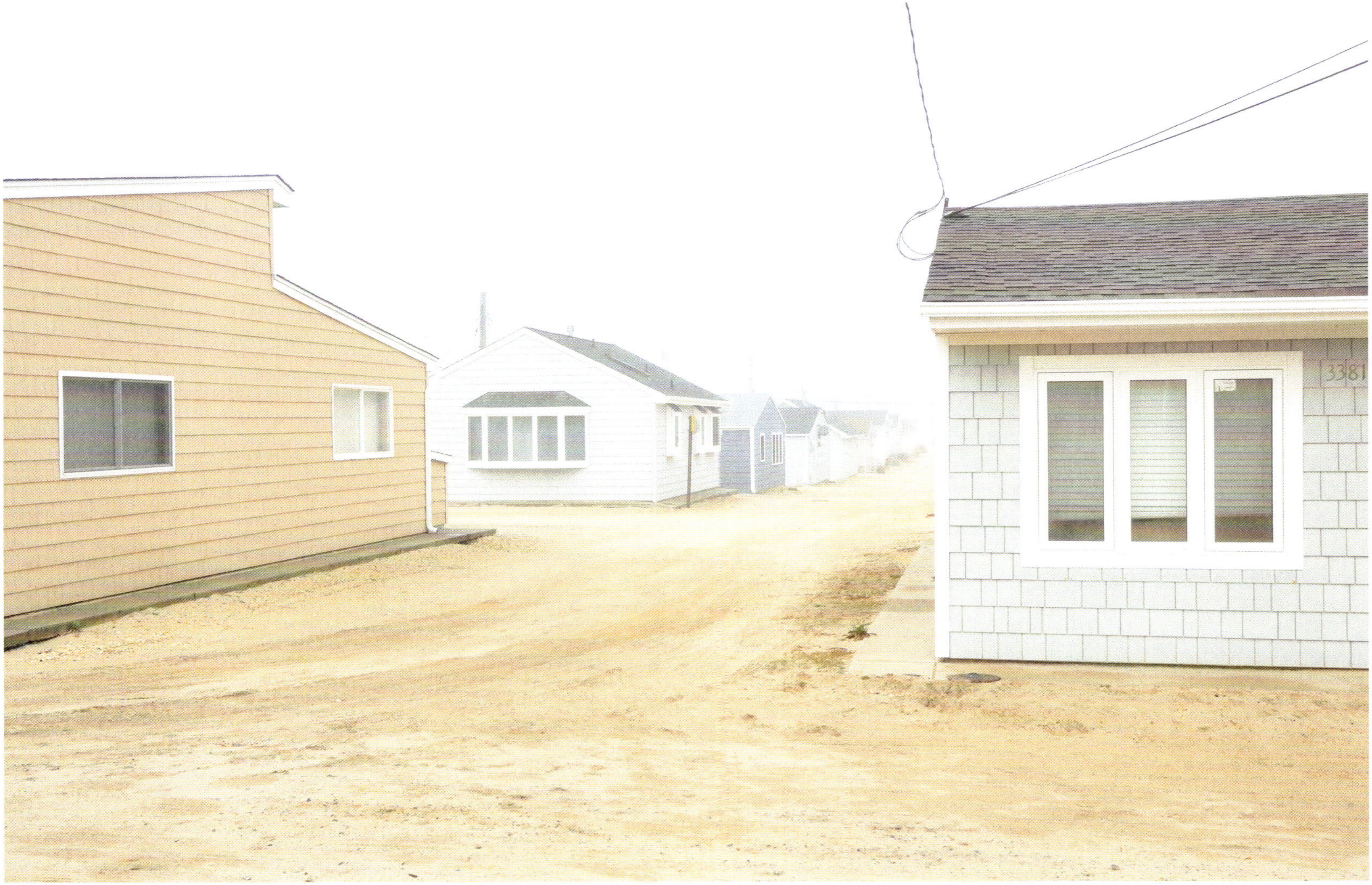
3381

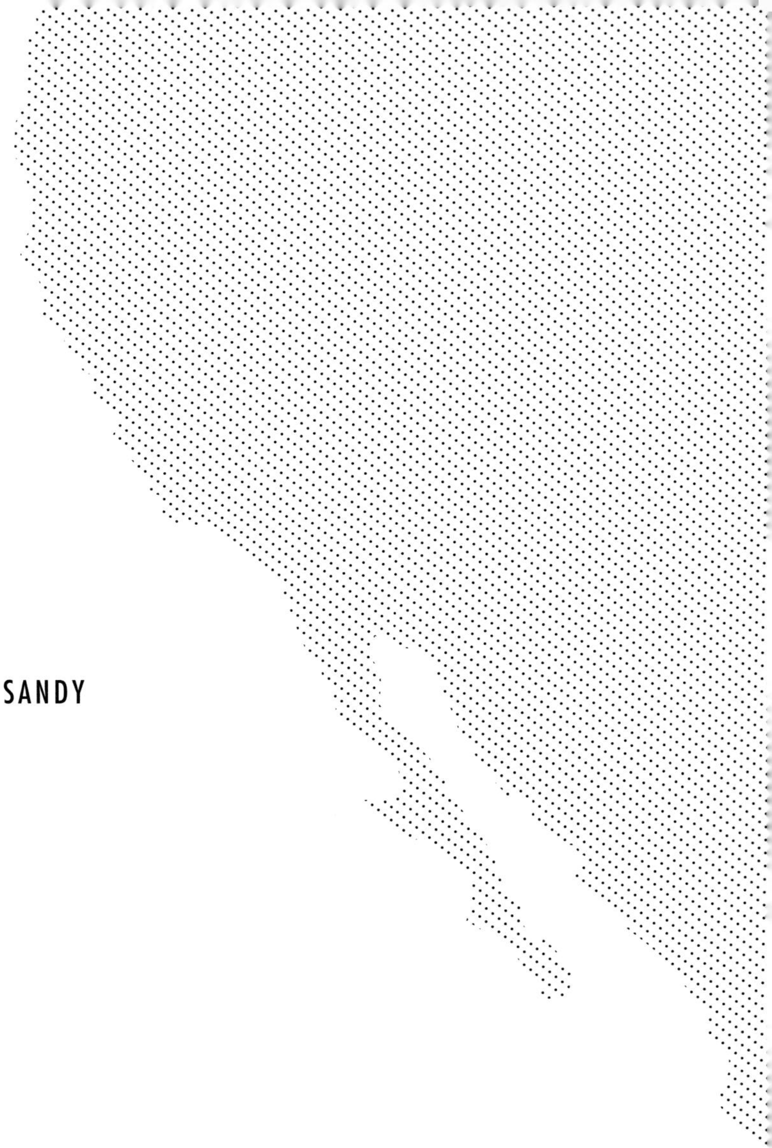

POST-HURRICANE SANDY

October 2012

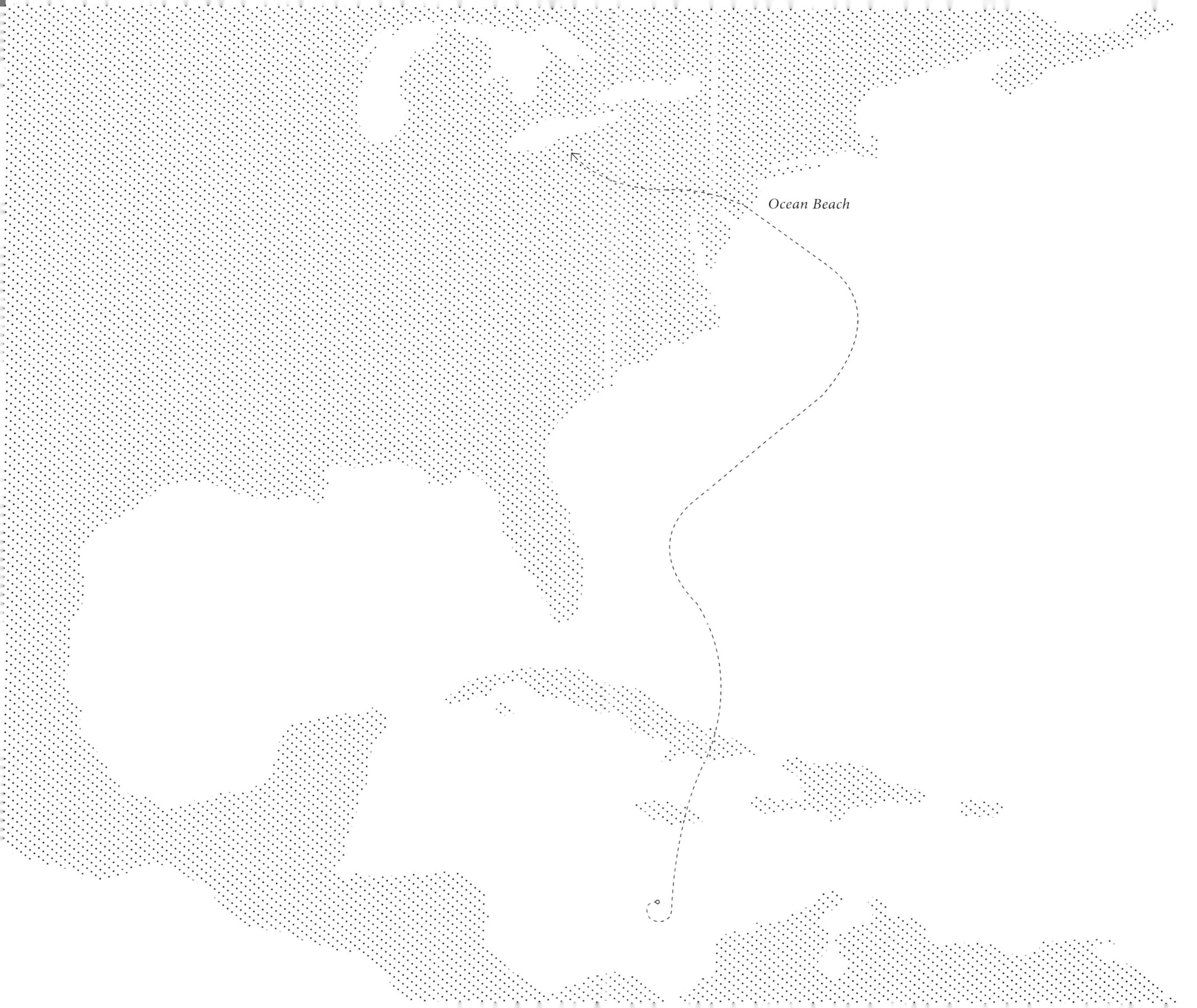
Ocean Beach

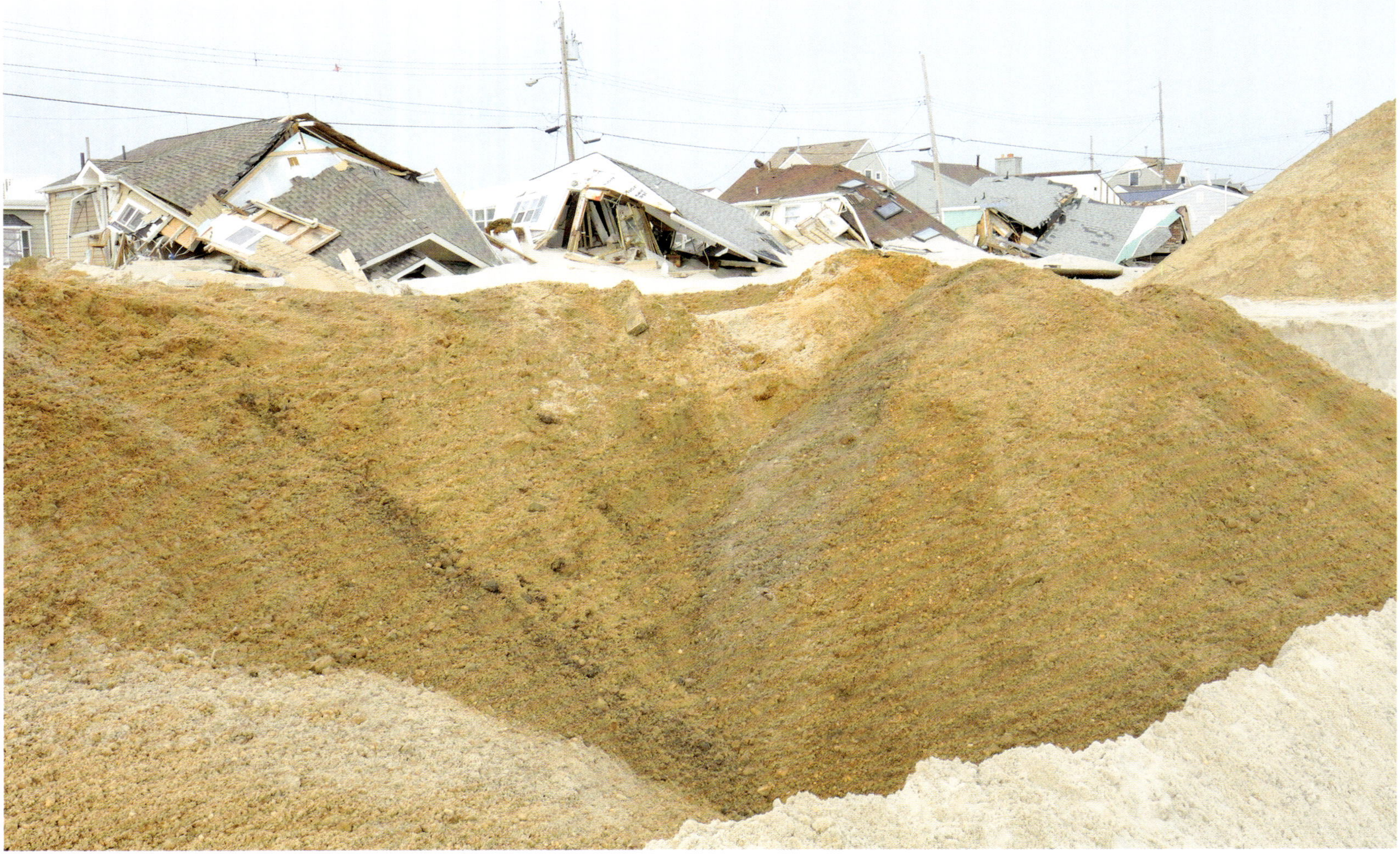

THE WEIGHT OF THINGS

A critical response to Douglas Ljungkvist's Ocean Beach

Steve Bisson

When looking at the images that complete the series, *Ocean Beach*, by photographer Douglas Ljungkvist, it is easy to find myself thinking about the following: the ruin of the American dream, the natural world reclaiming its spaces, or the humanist utopia of control over the earth's forces. All these considerations are inevitable but not decisive. First, it is interesting to recall the differences with the pre-hurricane series, which is certainly more descriptive. A more emphatic choice of colors reflects a deliberately darker mood. Even more significant is the decision to show in juxtaposition the housing wreckage and the natural elements of the landscape: the beach, the sky, and the sea. A contrast that cannot be seen, however, when the photographer has worked inside the remains of houses. It is then that the observer, with no means of escape, is forced to confront the inner dimension of destruction. It is in these shots that I feel all the uncertainty and fear of post-modern man. In fact, when I look at these images, I am projected far beyond a possible commentary on the medium or the wish to classify the work within a discourse on photography. I see rather, in this second part of Douglas Ljungkvist's work, a centrifugal force that propels one's gaze out of the aesthetic dimension. In this sense, I do not think it useful to recall the ideas surrounding *New Topographics*. Instead, I find it pertinent to turn my thoughts to the deconstruction axioms or the ›building cuts‹ of Gordon Matta-Clark. This series of images is a real détournement, a state that is antithetical to a thought of origin, being a recycling of pre-existing artistic elements into a new form. The photographer works, more or less consciously, on a re-contextualization. It is no longer important to point out which elements are in opposition or why. We need to understand what new meanings emerge from these realities, because their future inheres in their irreducible and irremediable coexistence. I have the impression that this work effectively makes manifest the illusory aspirations and the comfort fetishism of the modern age. In the words of Guy Debord, »everything directly lived has receded into representation.« Ljungkvist inevitably prompts us to question our notions of the real rather than considering the role of the photographer. From this point of view, I appreciate the photographer's detachment from the implied compassion that often hovers around such situations. The decision not to include human beings gives this work the distance necessary to prevent the process of identification with place and instead feeds a sense of alienation. We cannot conclude this brief critical reading without expressing the need to present a dualistic-semiotics reading of the images, in order to grasp those signs that express cultural phenomena. In this sense, Douglas Ljungkvist is skilled at presenting the attentive viewer, in an unprejudiced way, with a useful anthropological summary of Western consumer society; throughout, we see its fragile precariousness and all its superficial fun. From this perspective, might what we see also be a symbolic reaction to the ongoing expansion of the world based on the exploitation of its resources? In other words, have these homes been destroyed by a natural disaster or by their own weight?

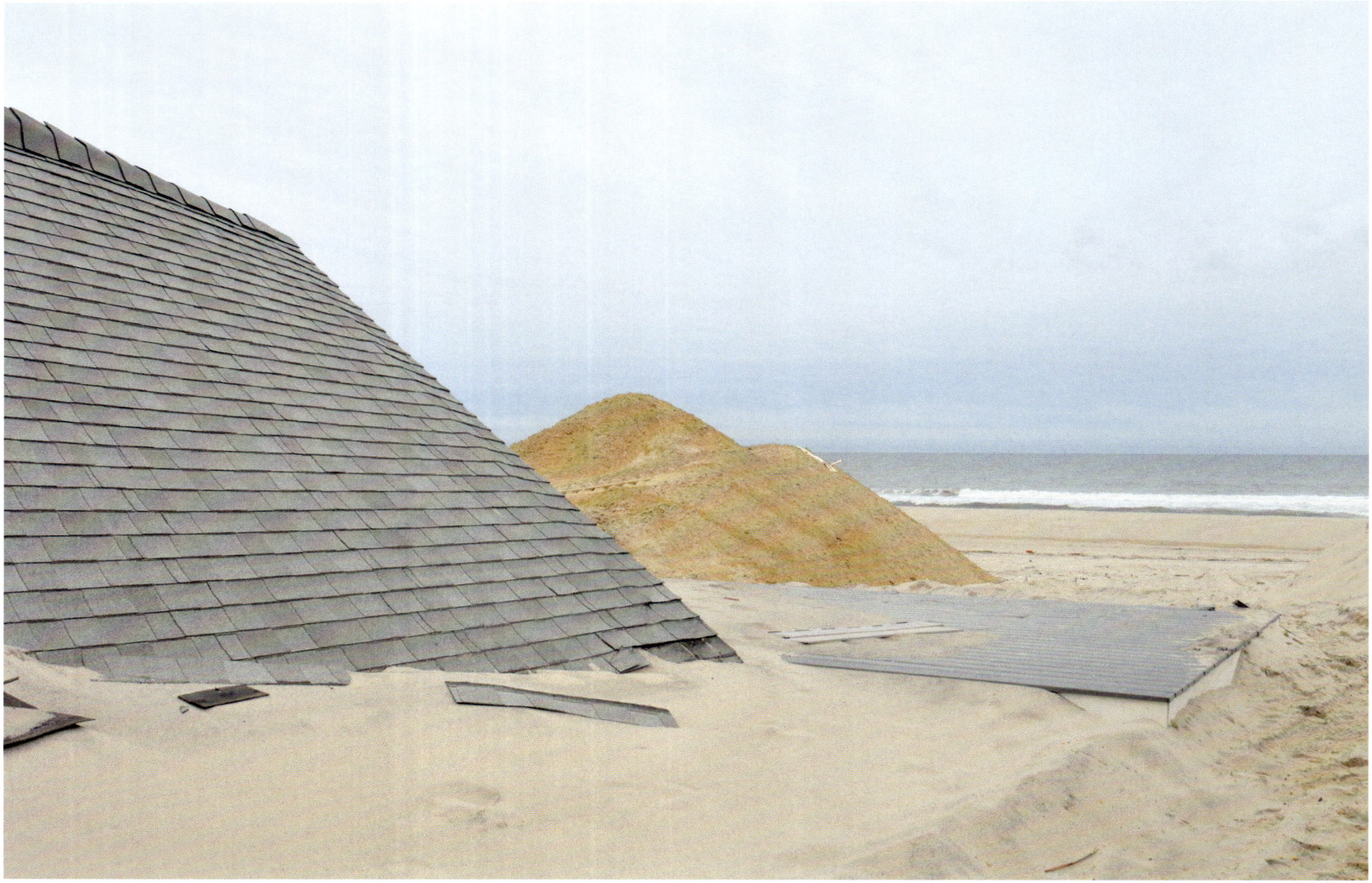

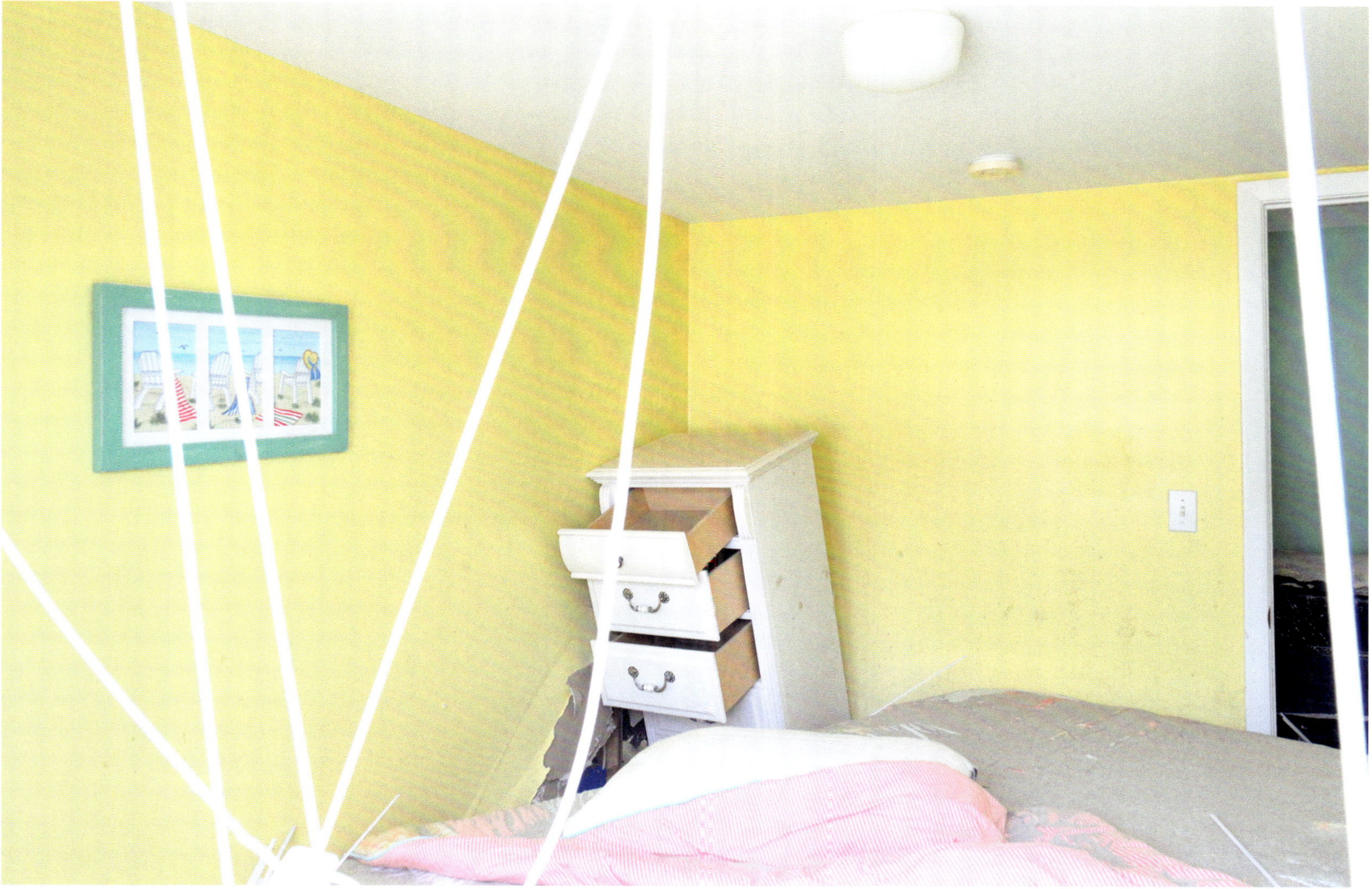

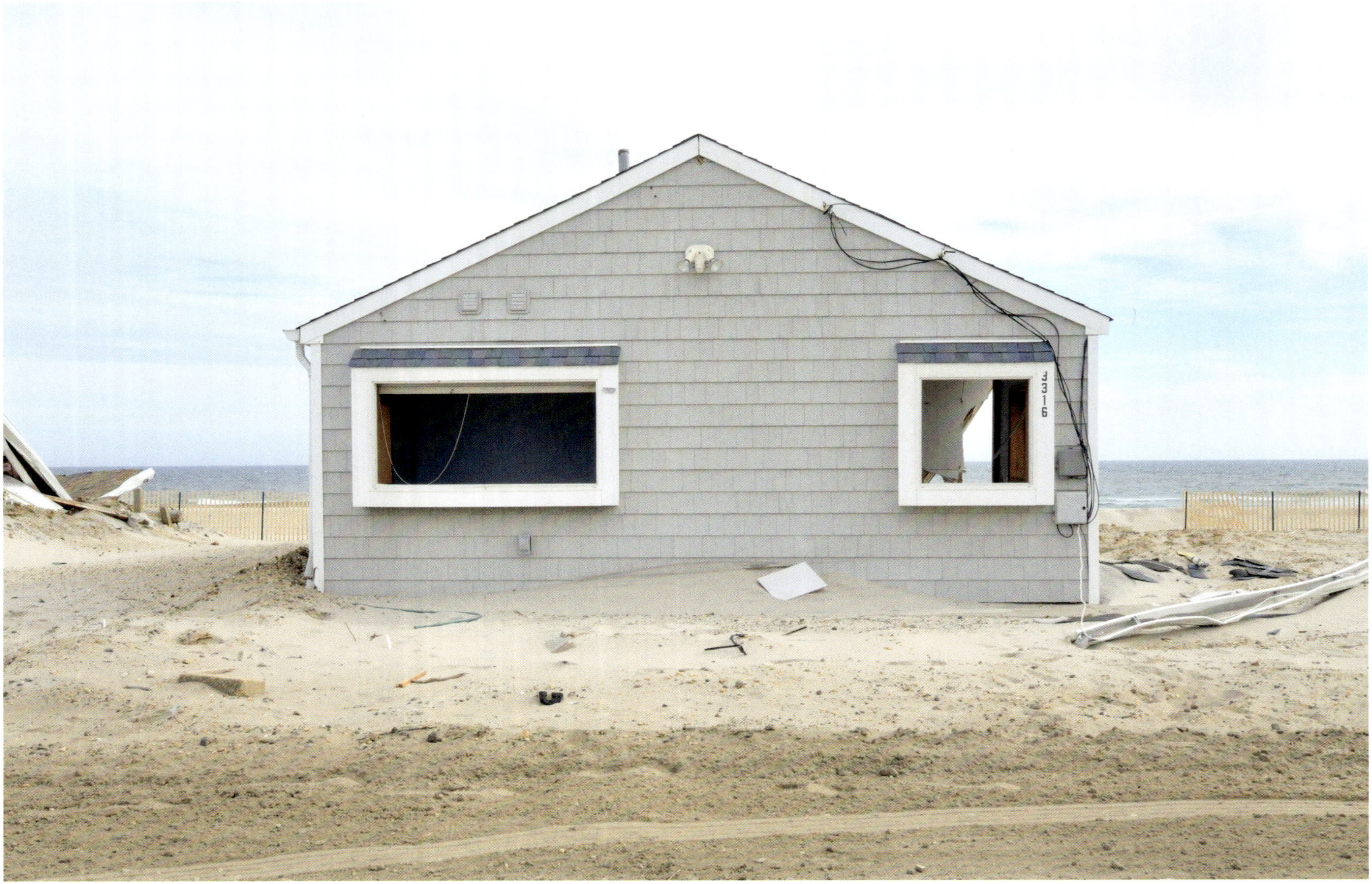
3316

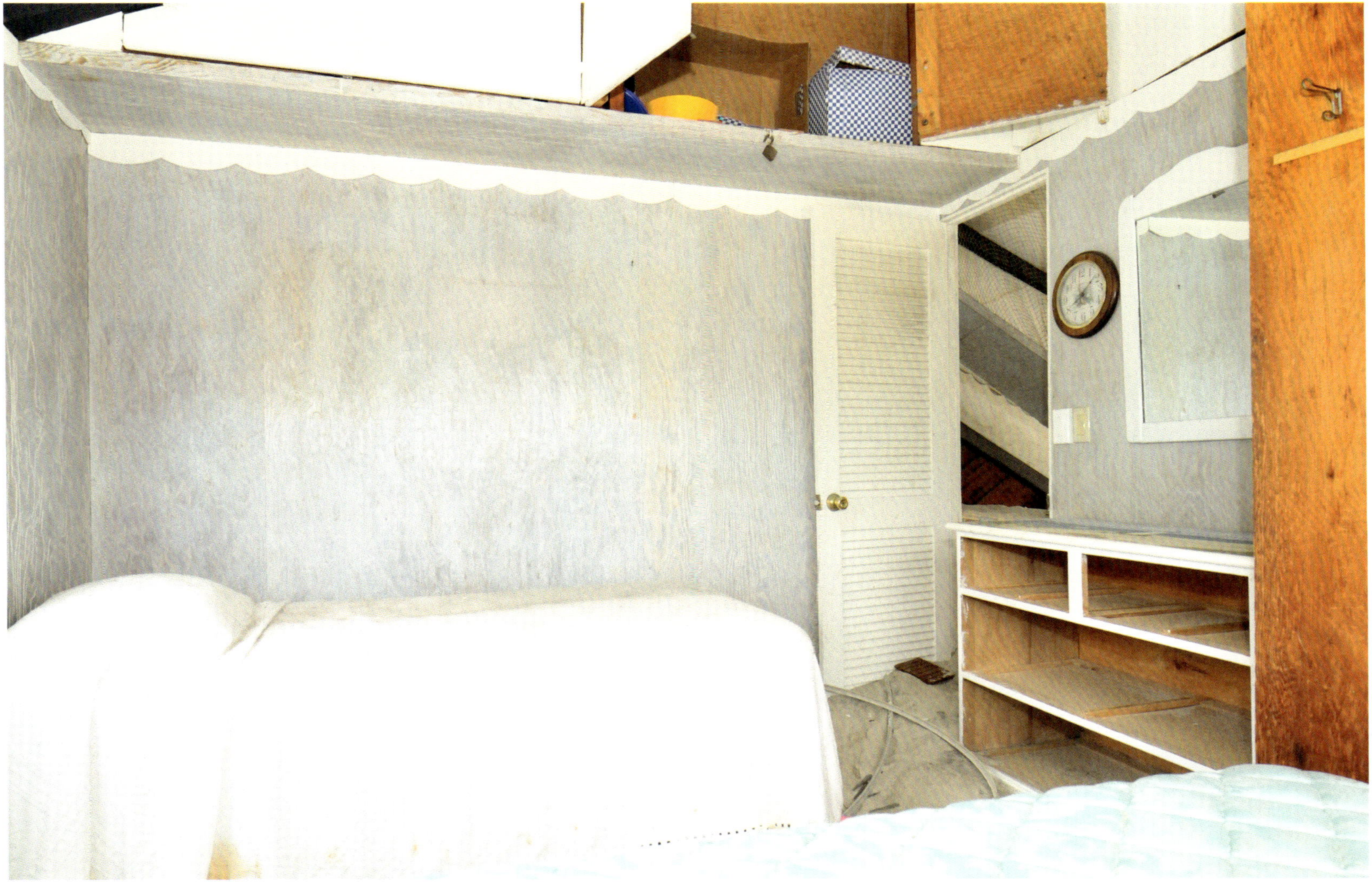

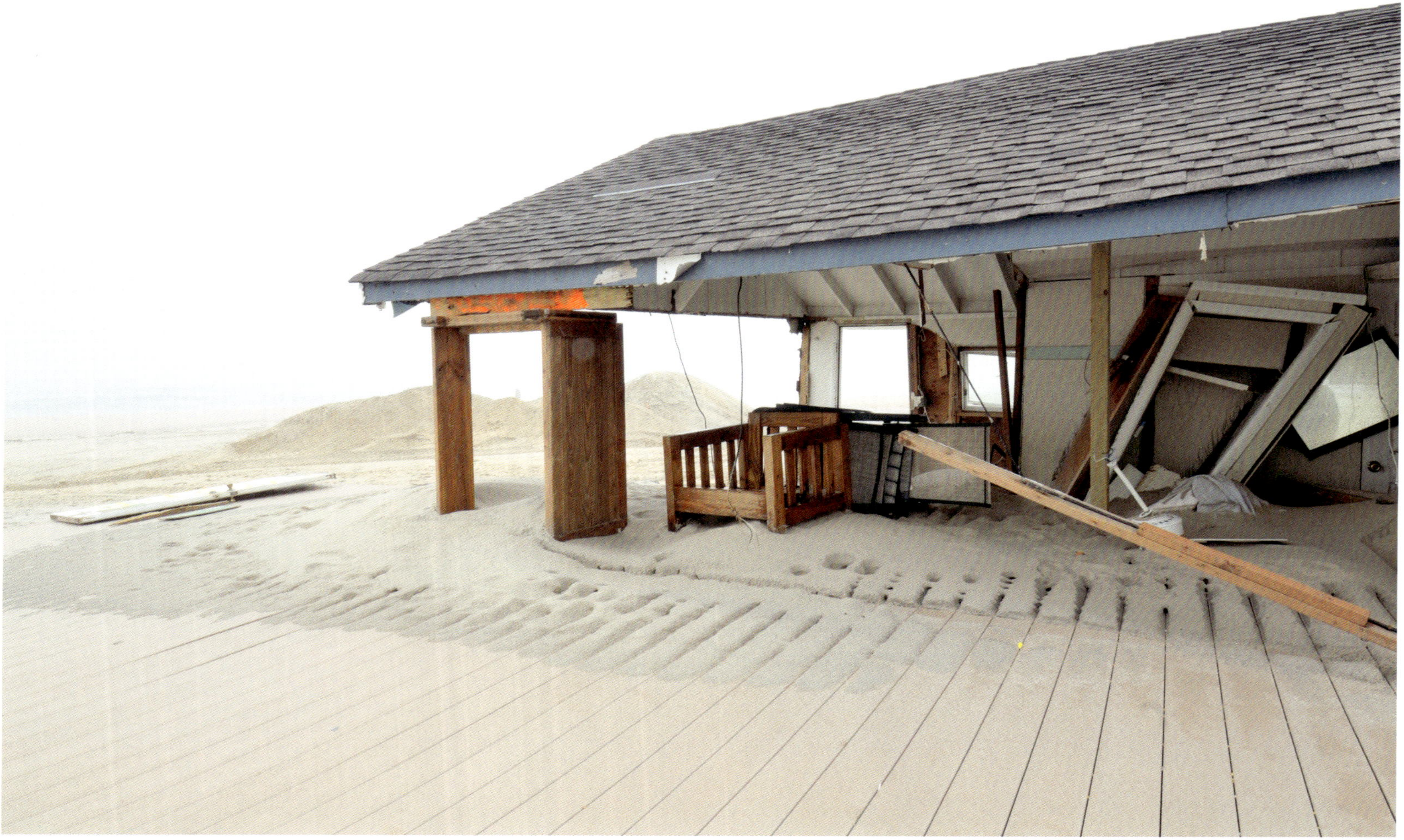

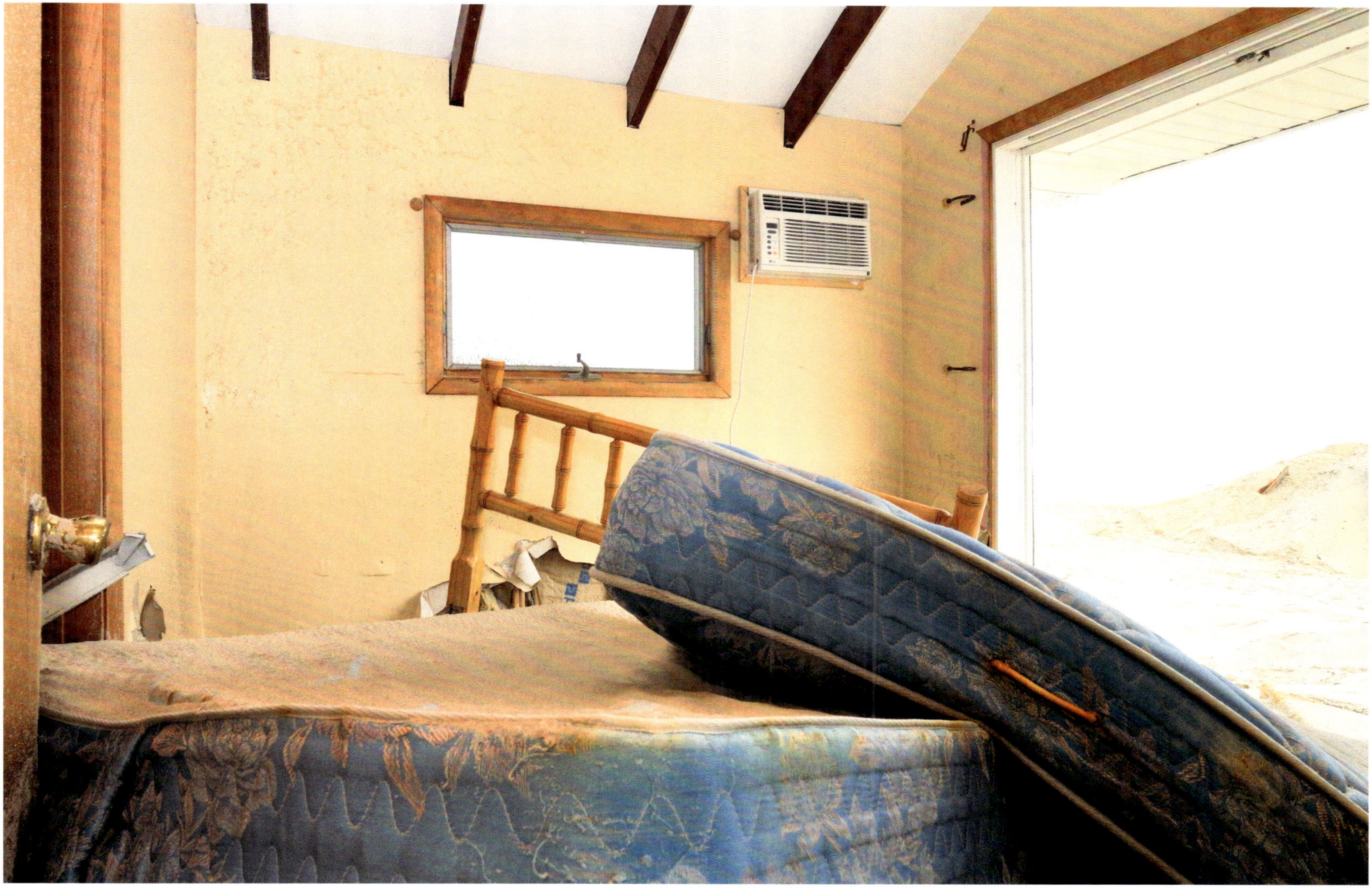

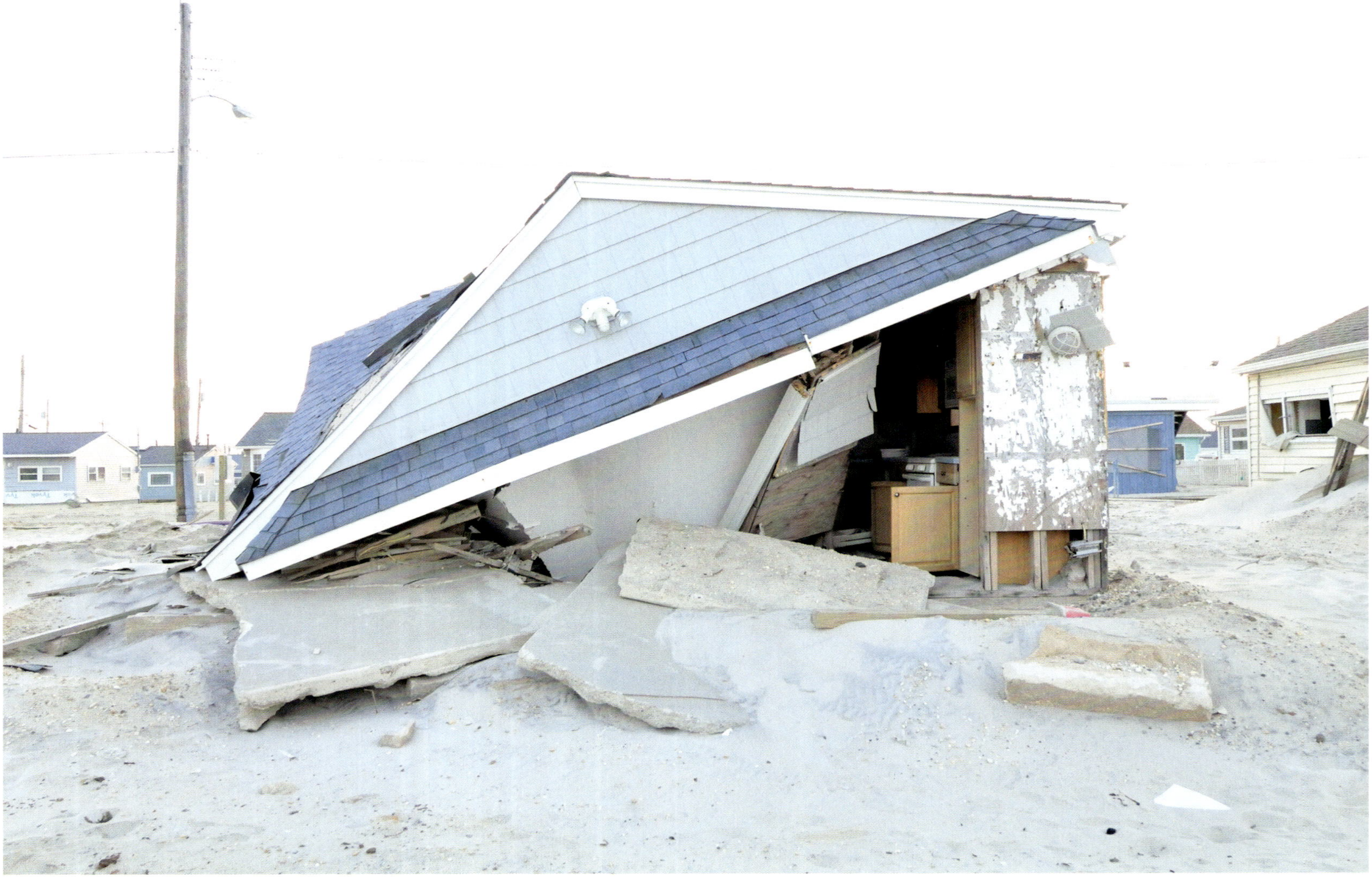

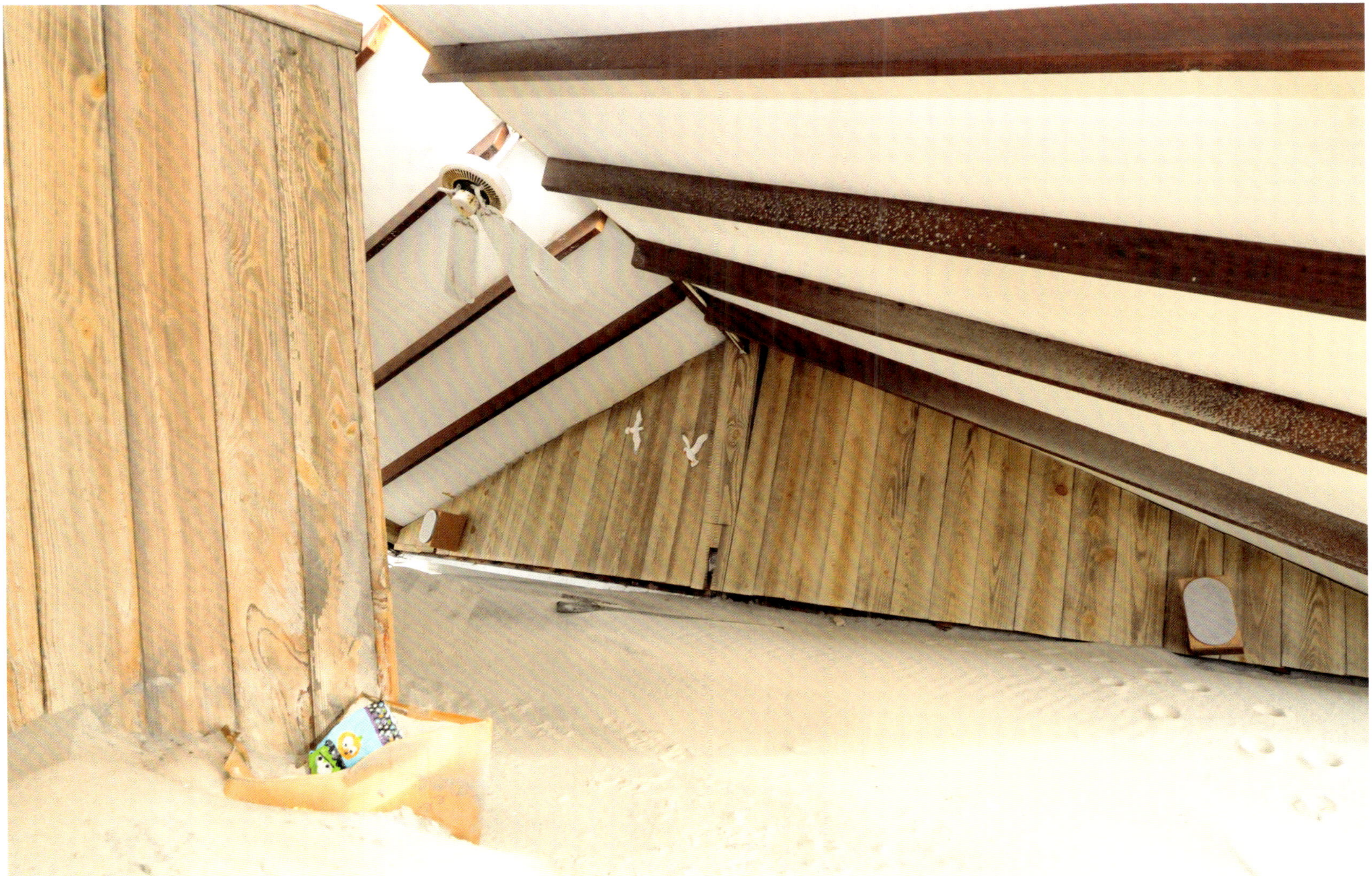

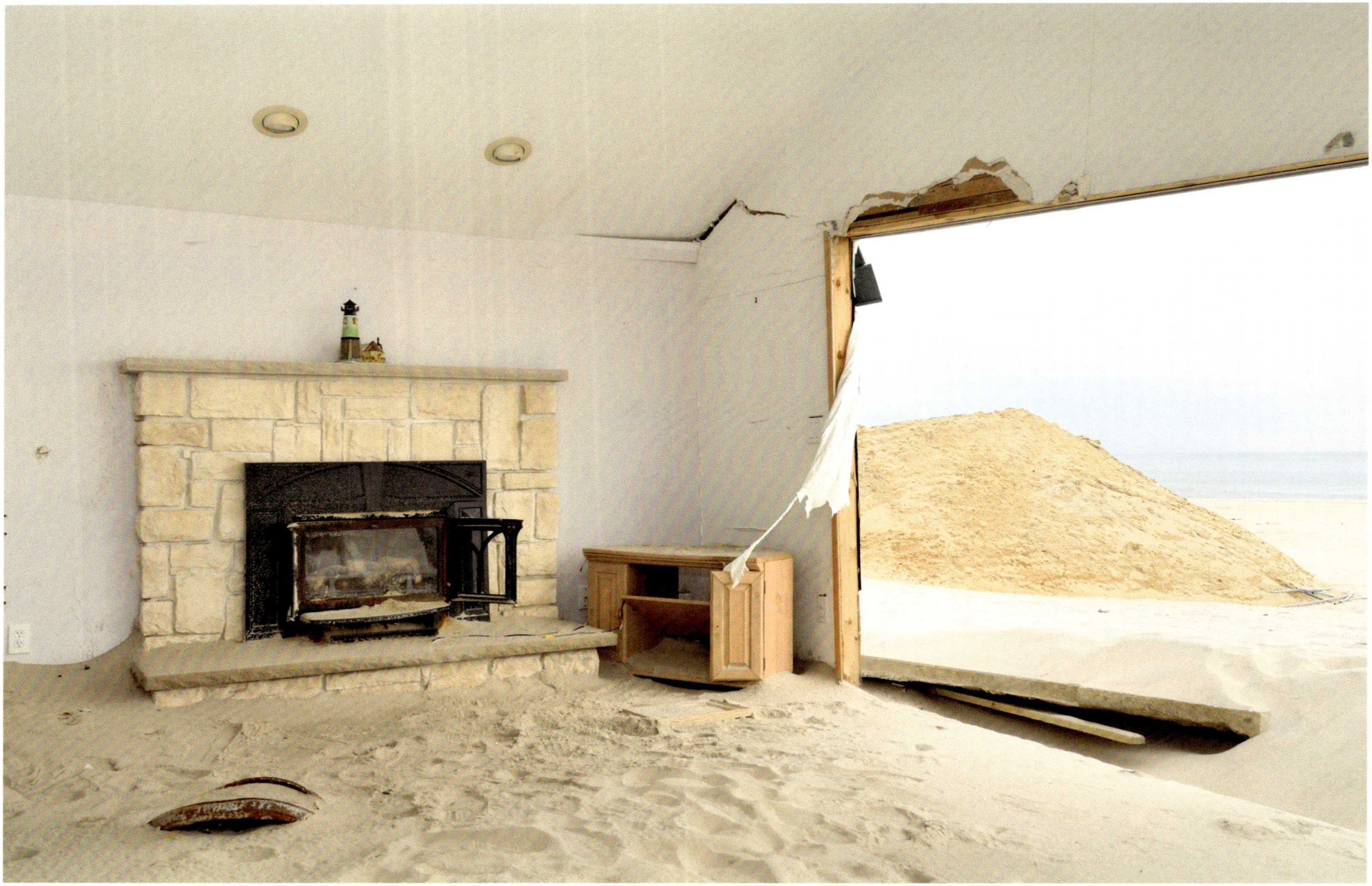

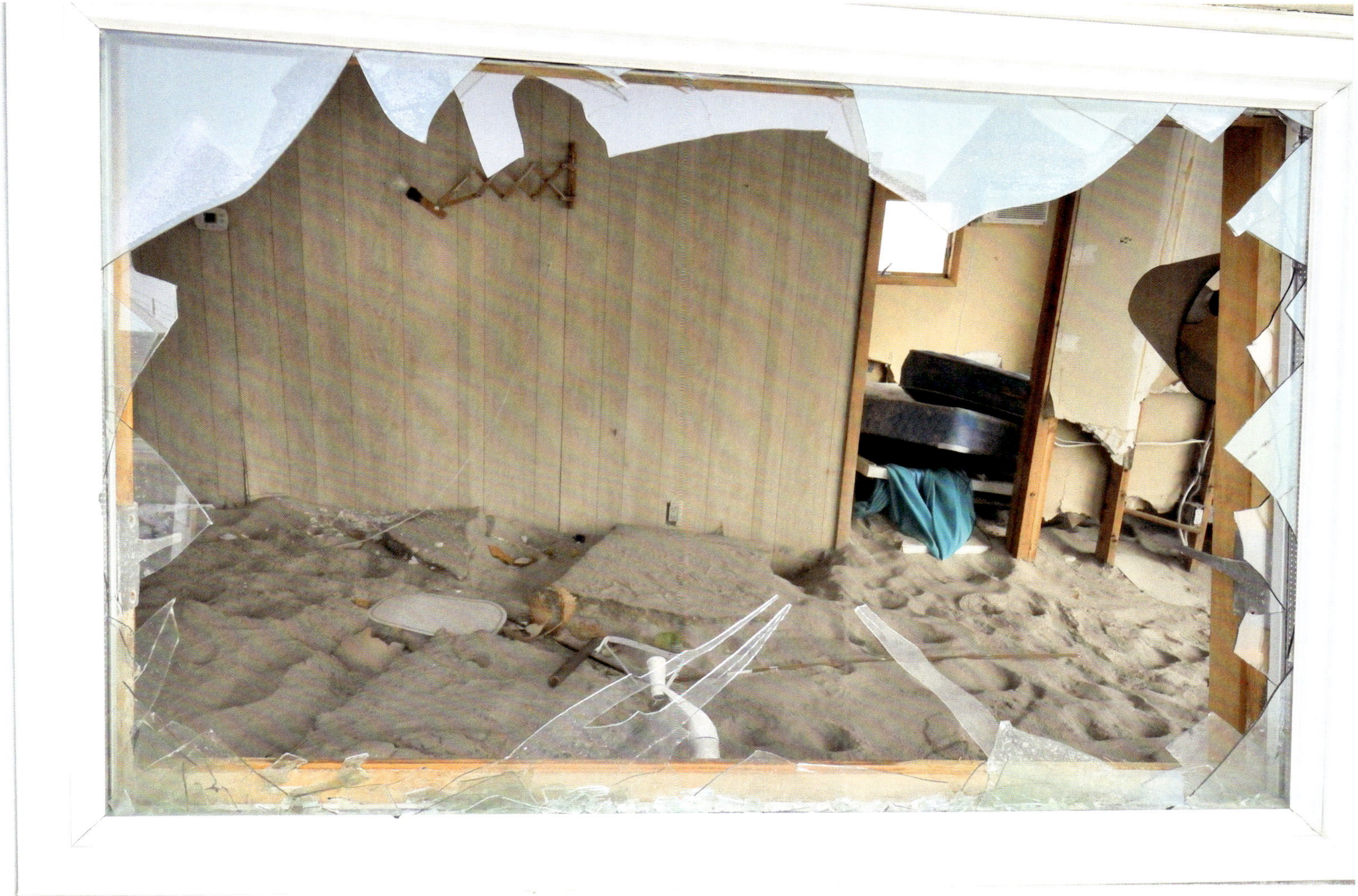

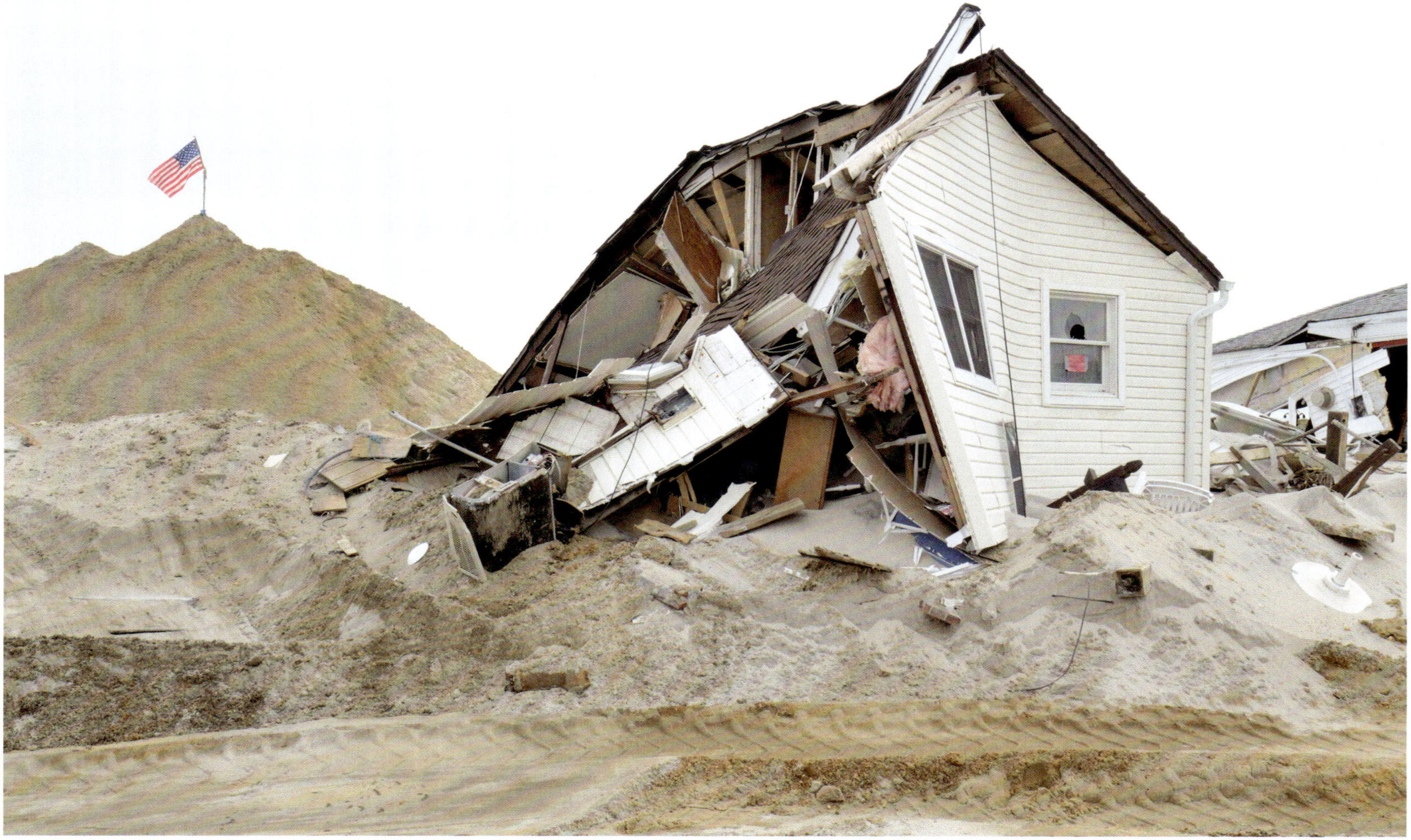

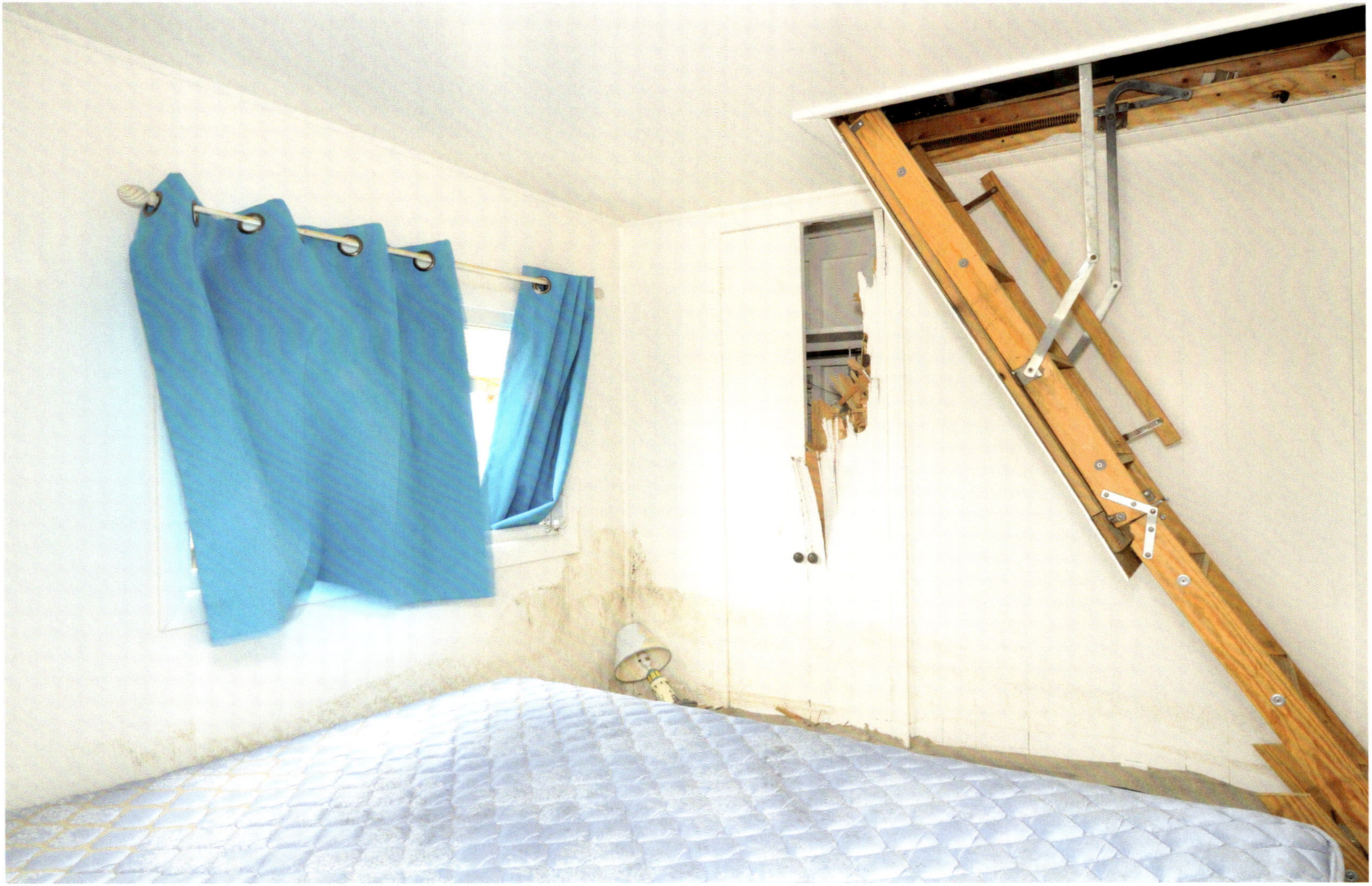

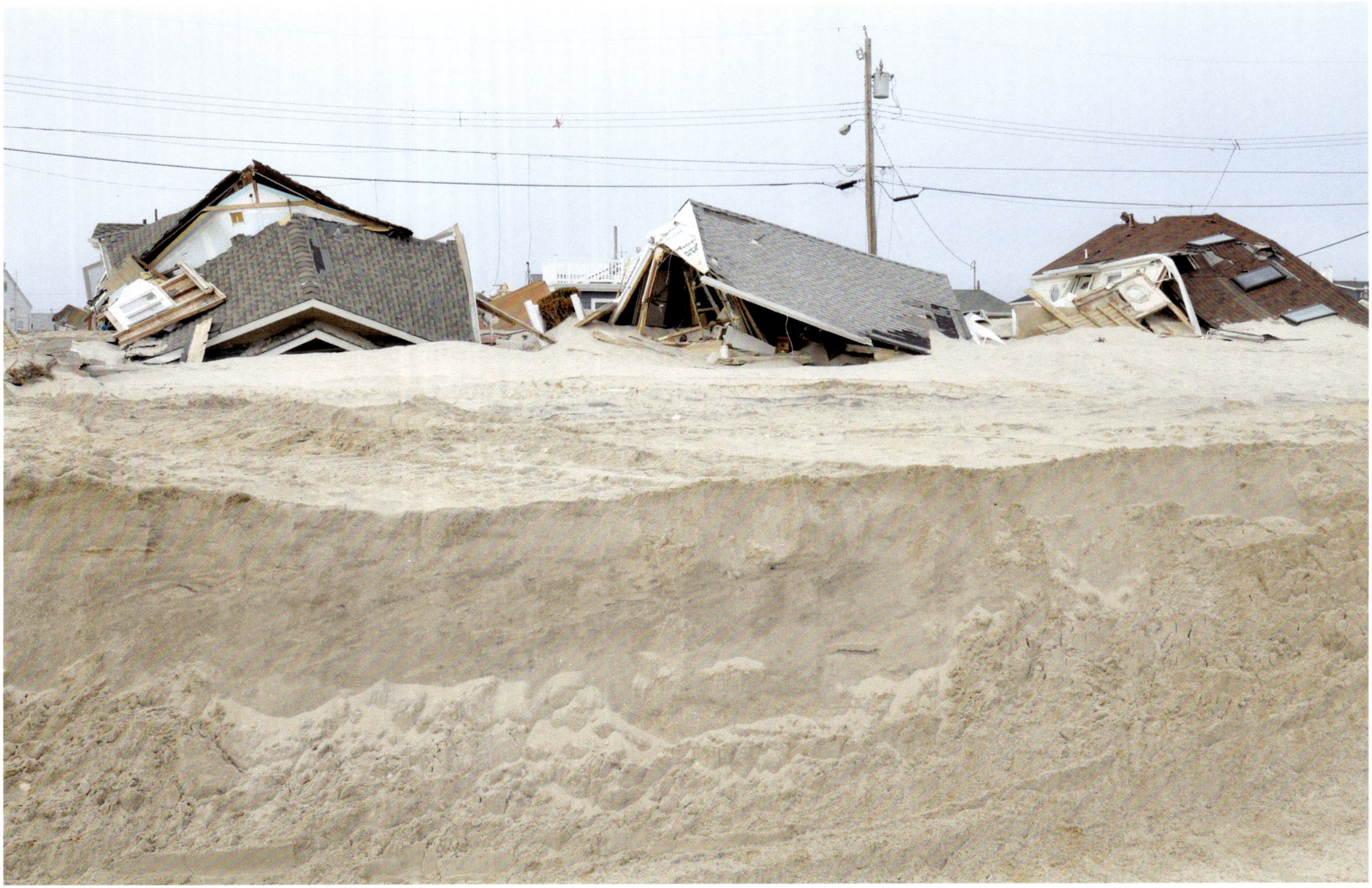

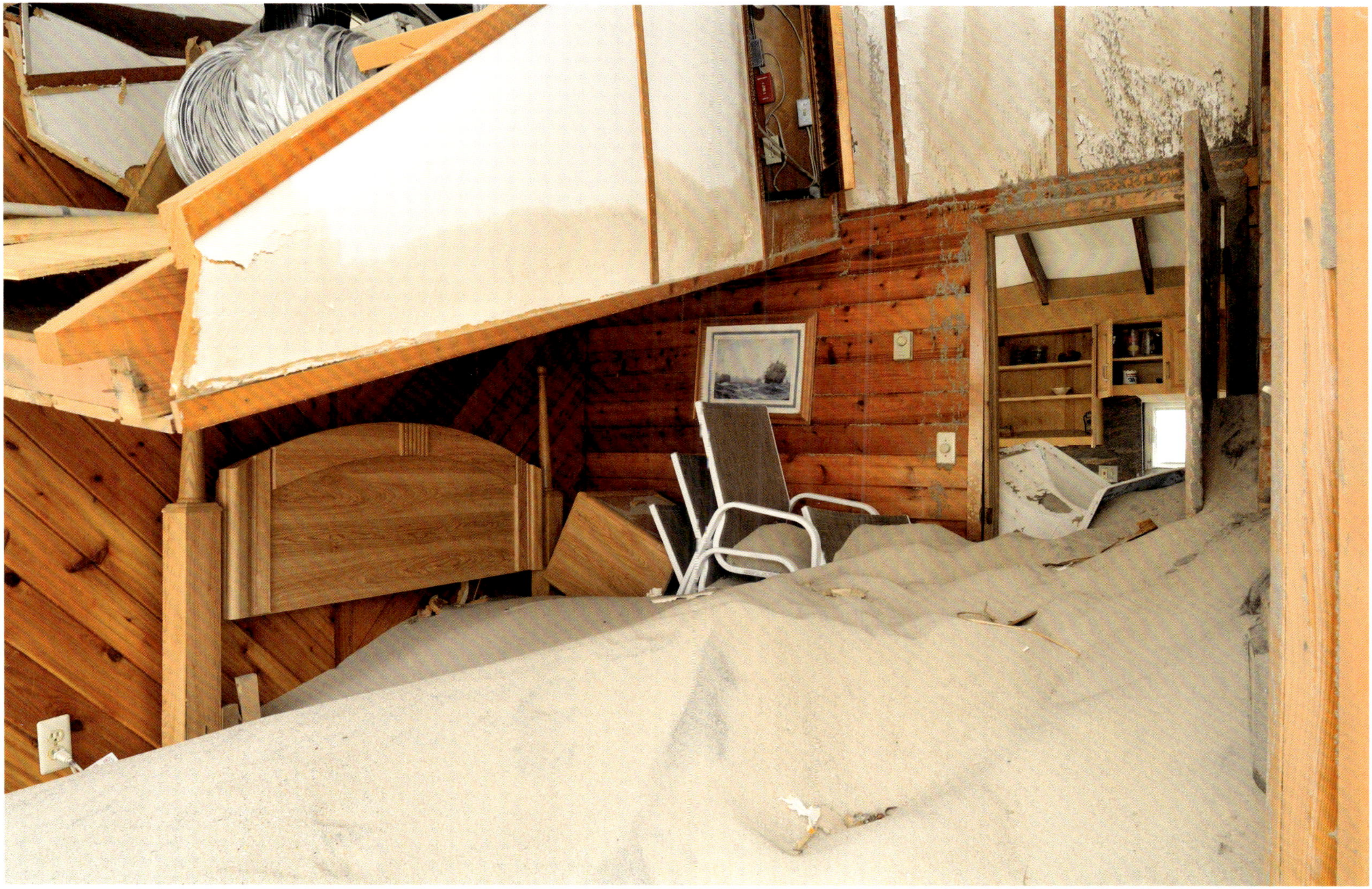

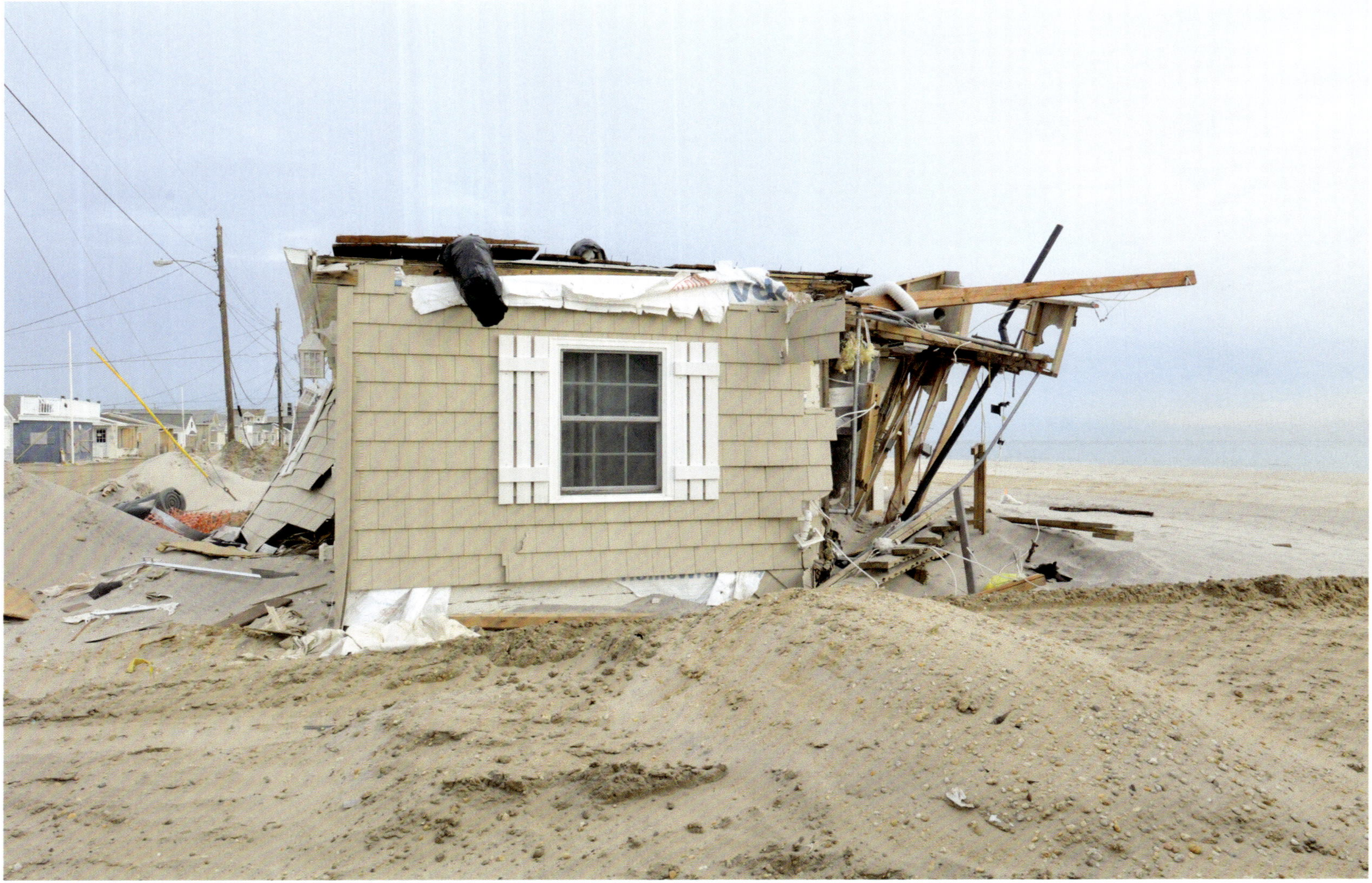

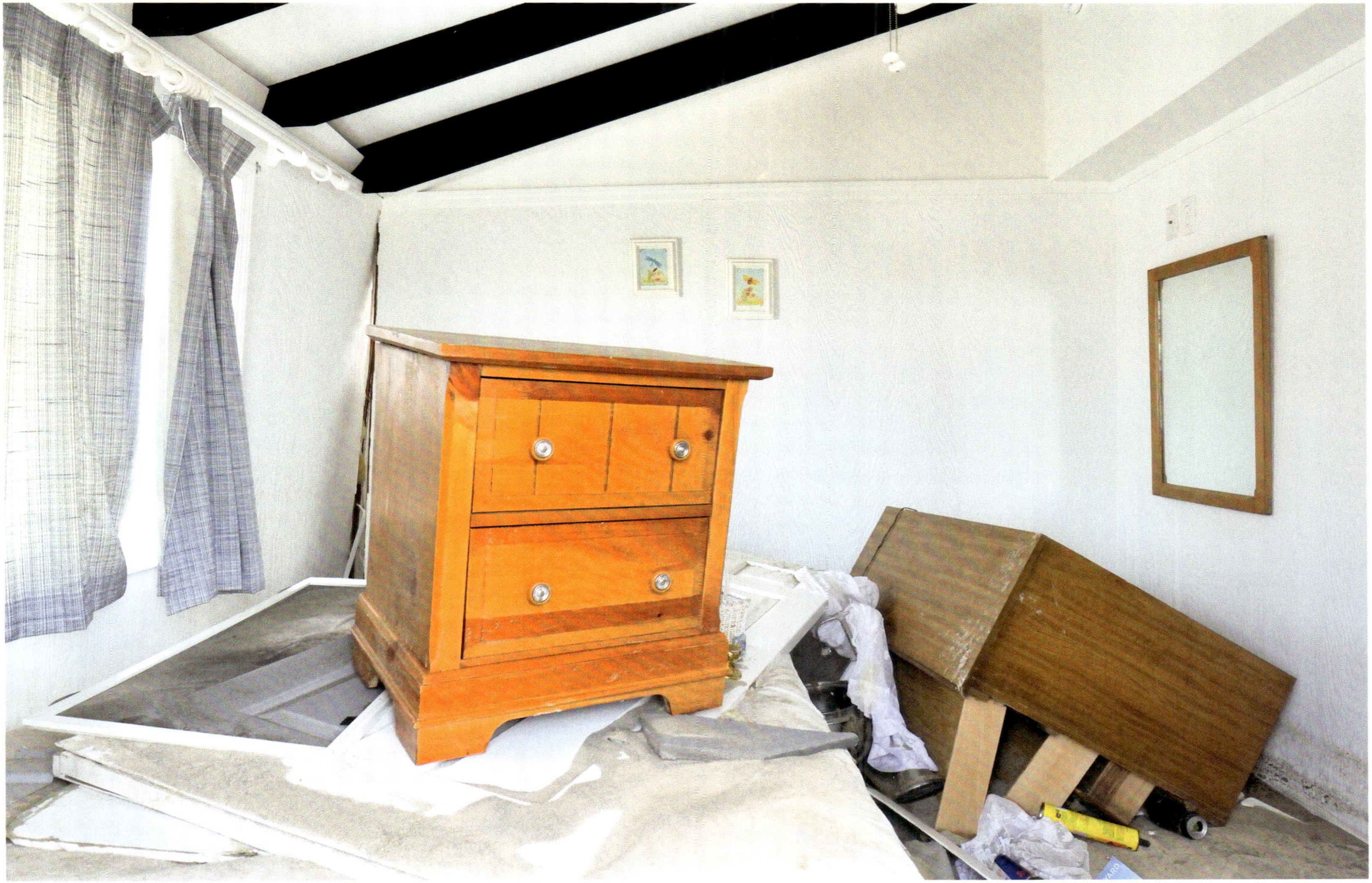

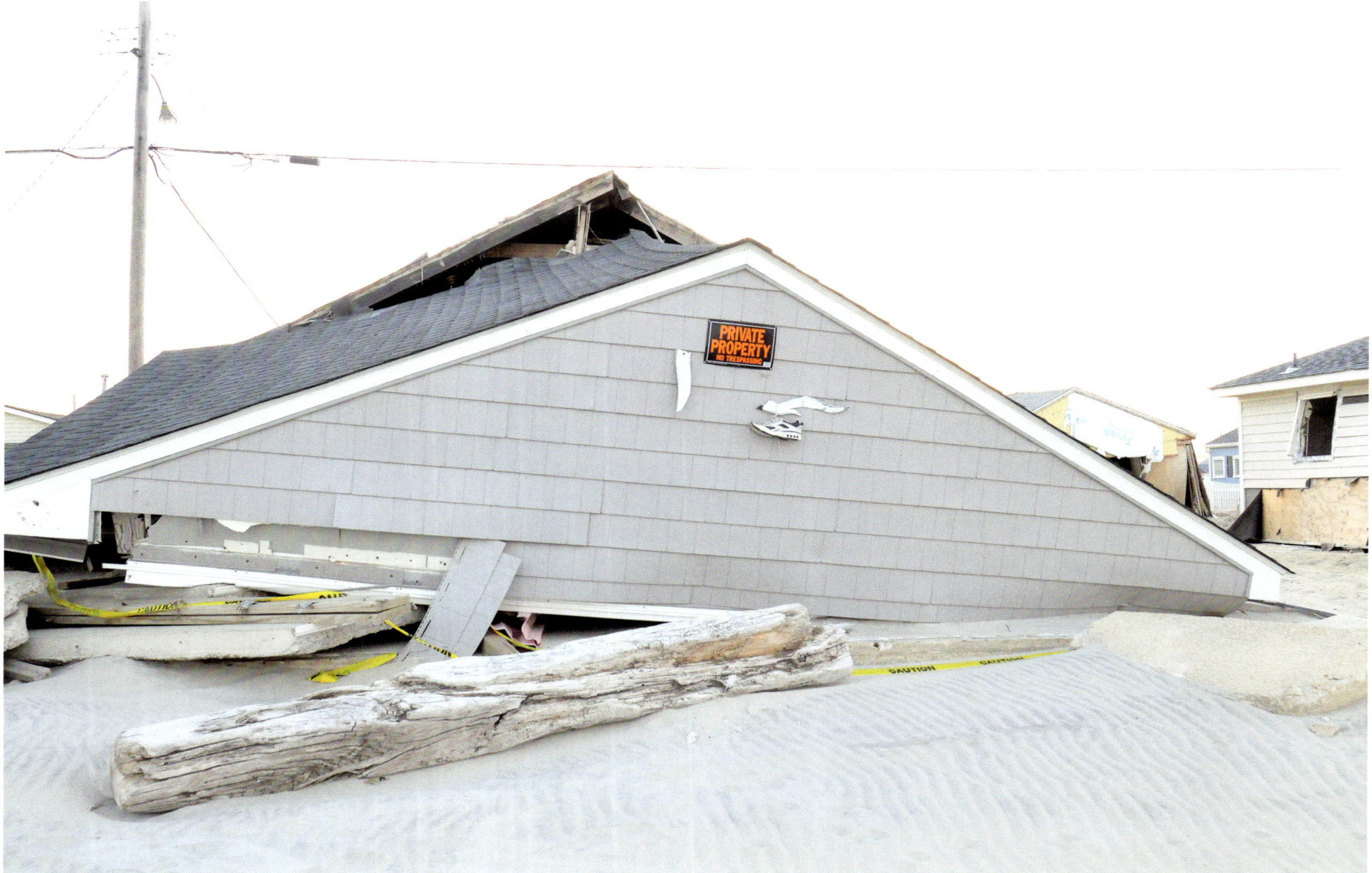
PRIVATE
PROPERTY
NO TRESPASSING

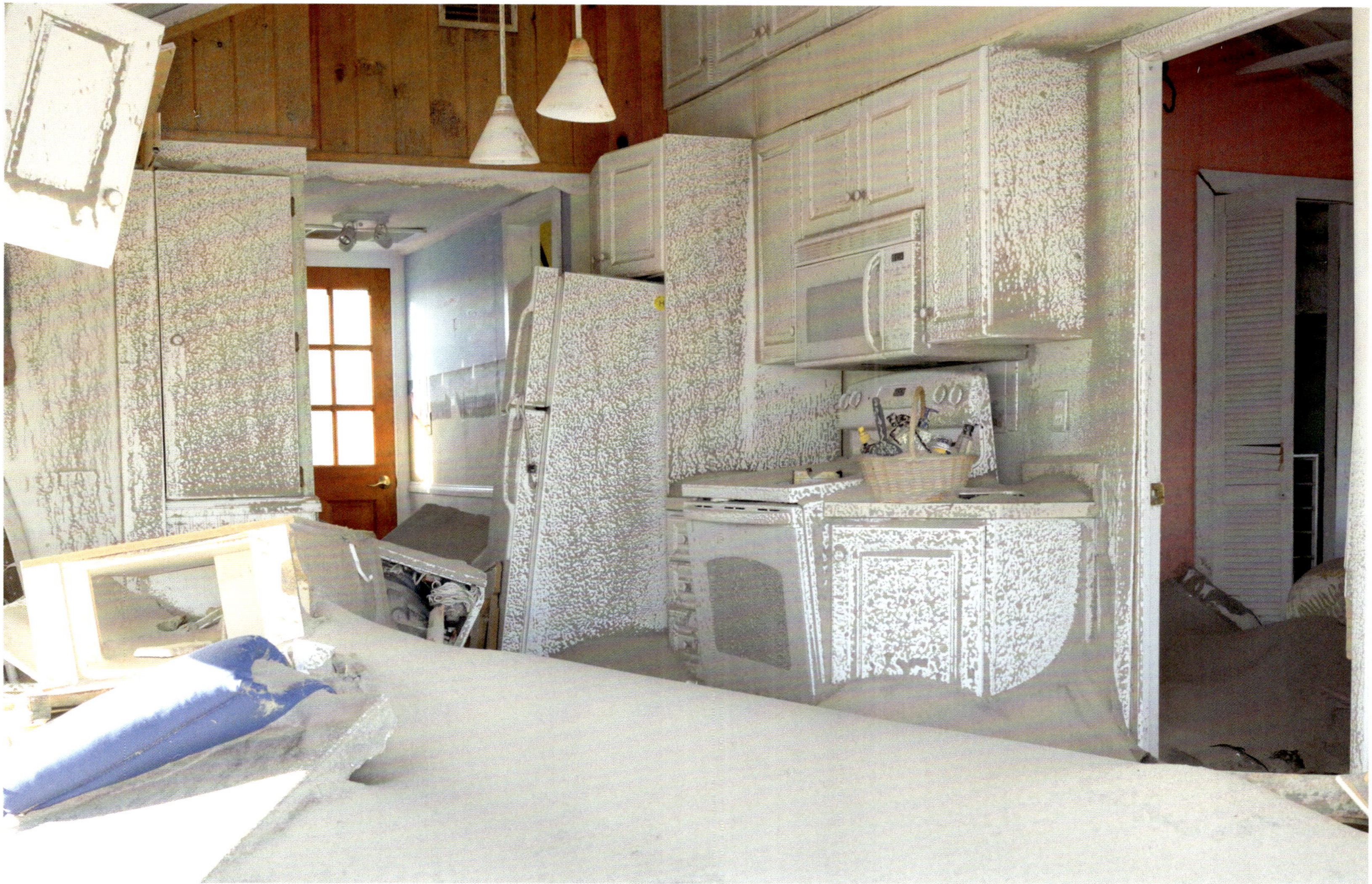

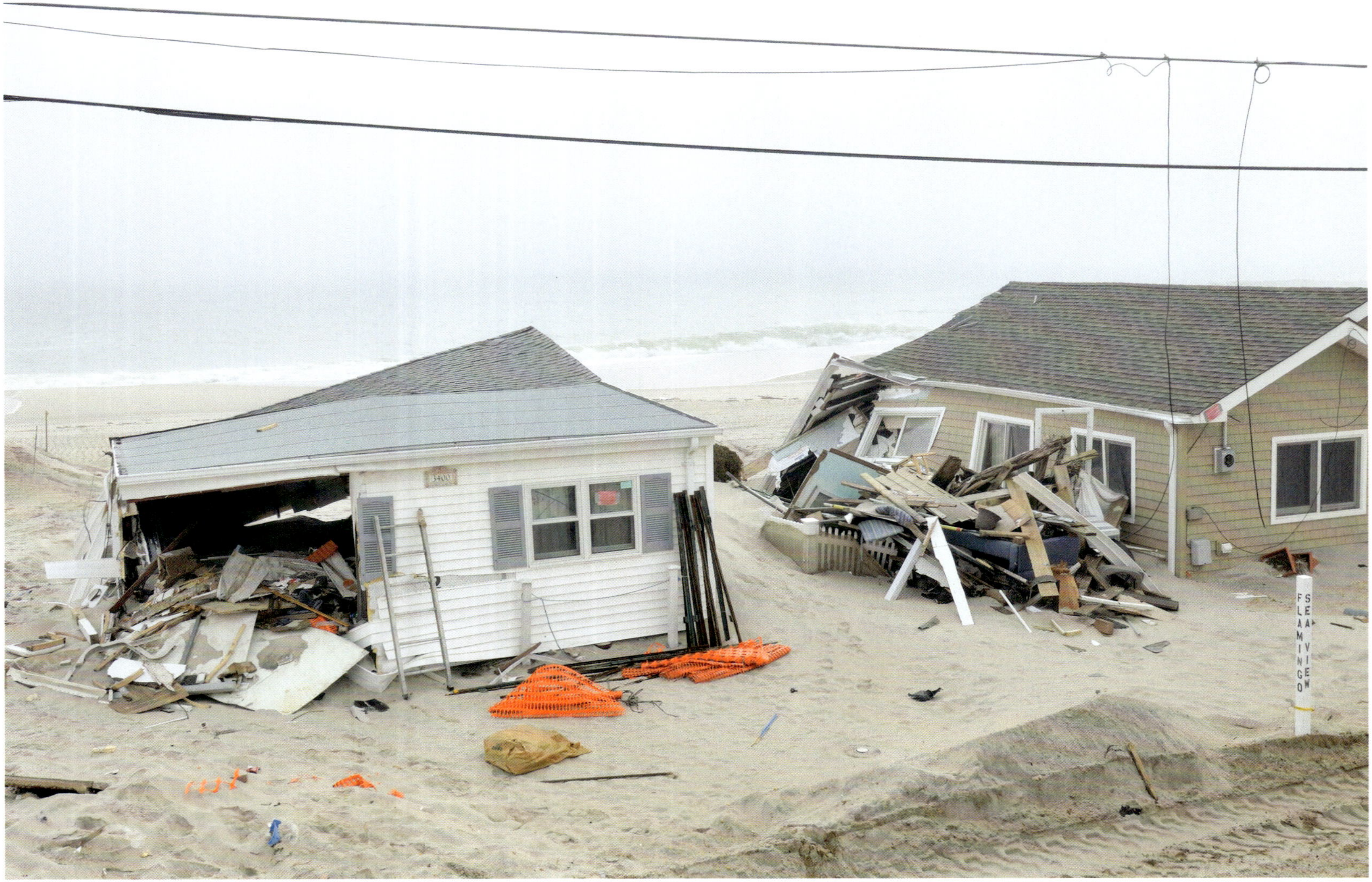
SEAVIEW
FLAMINGO

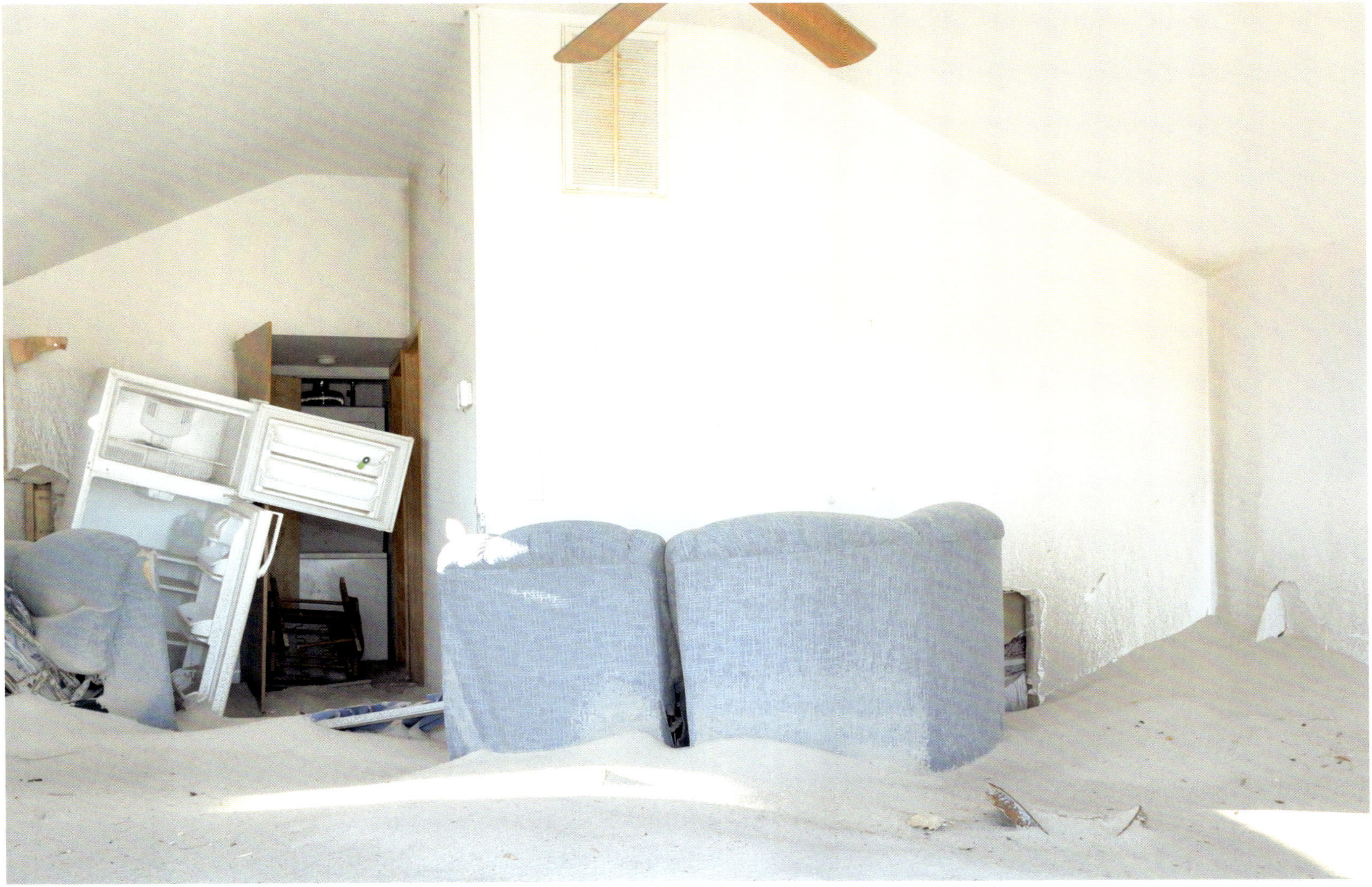

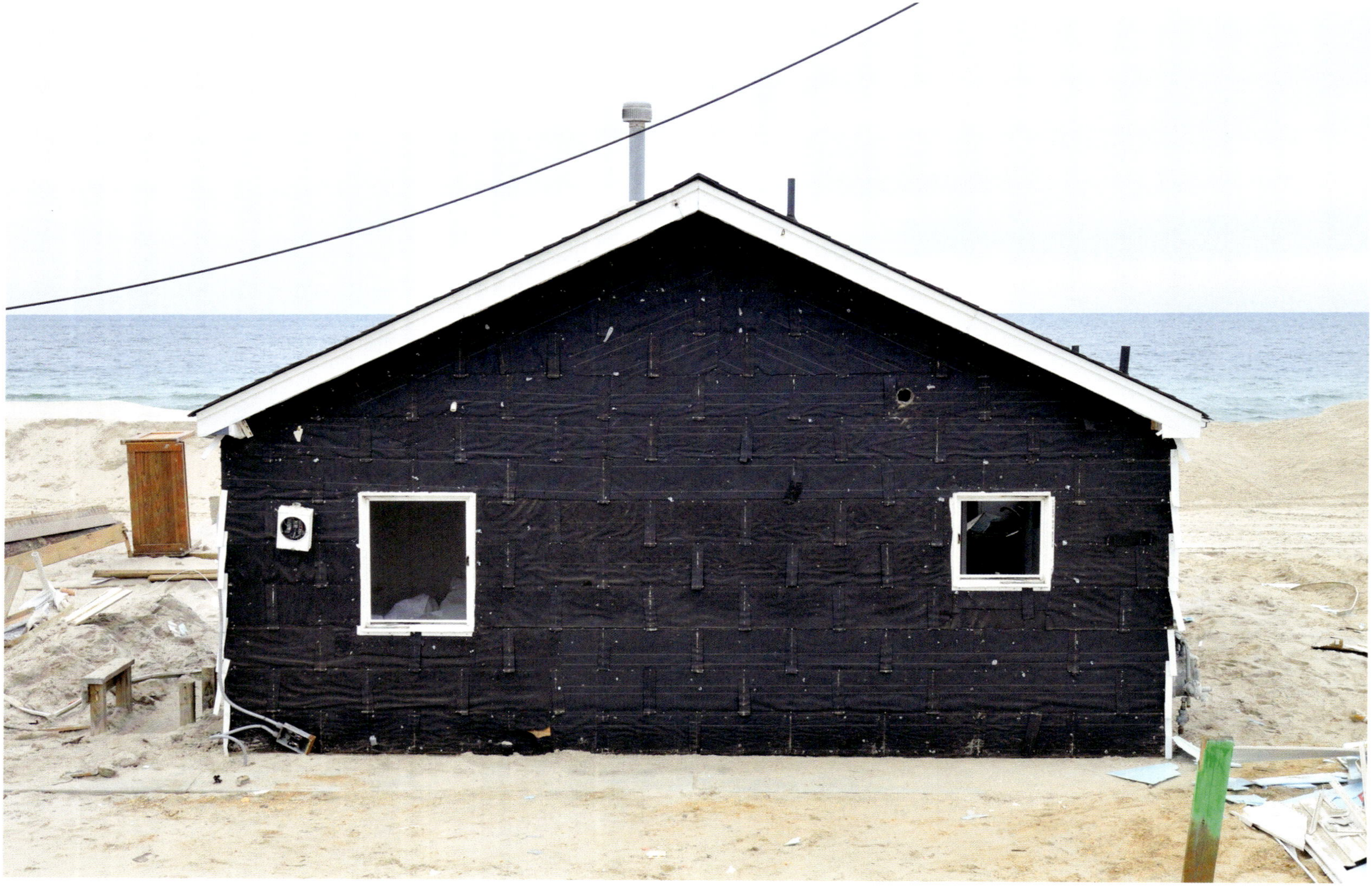

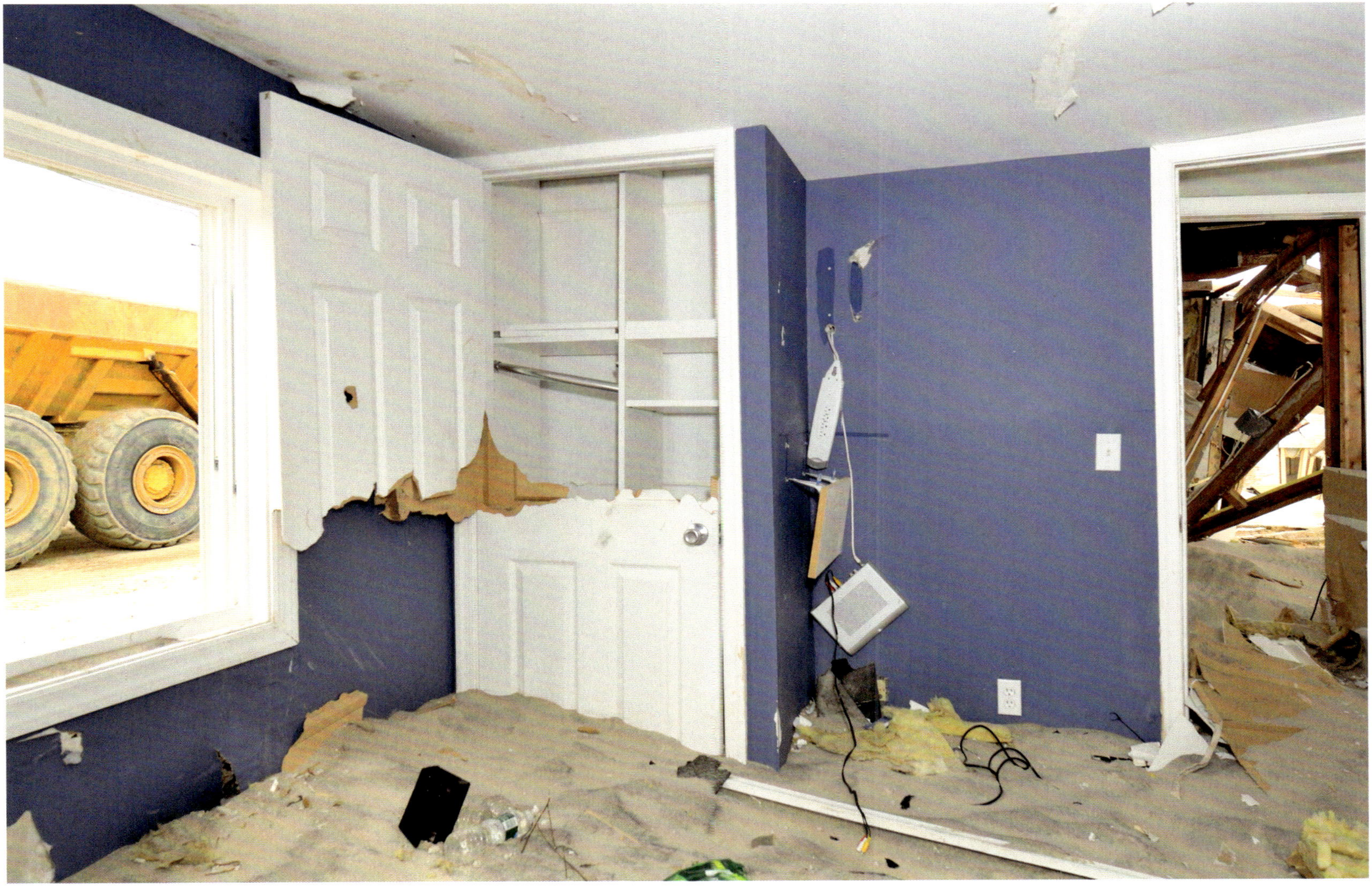

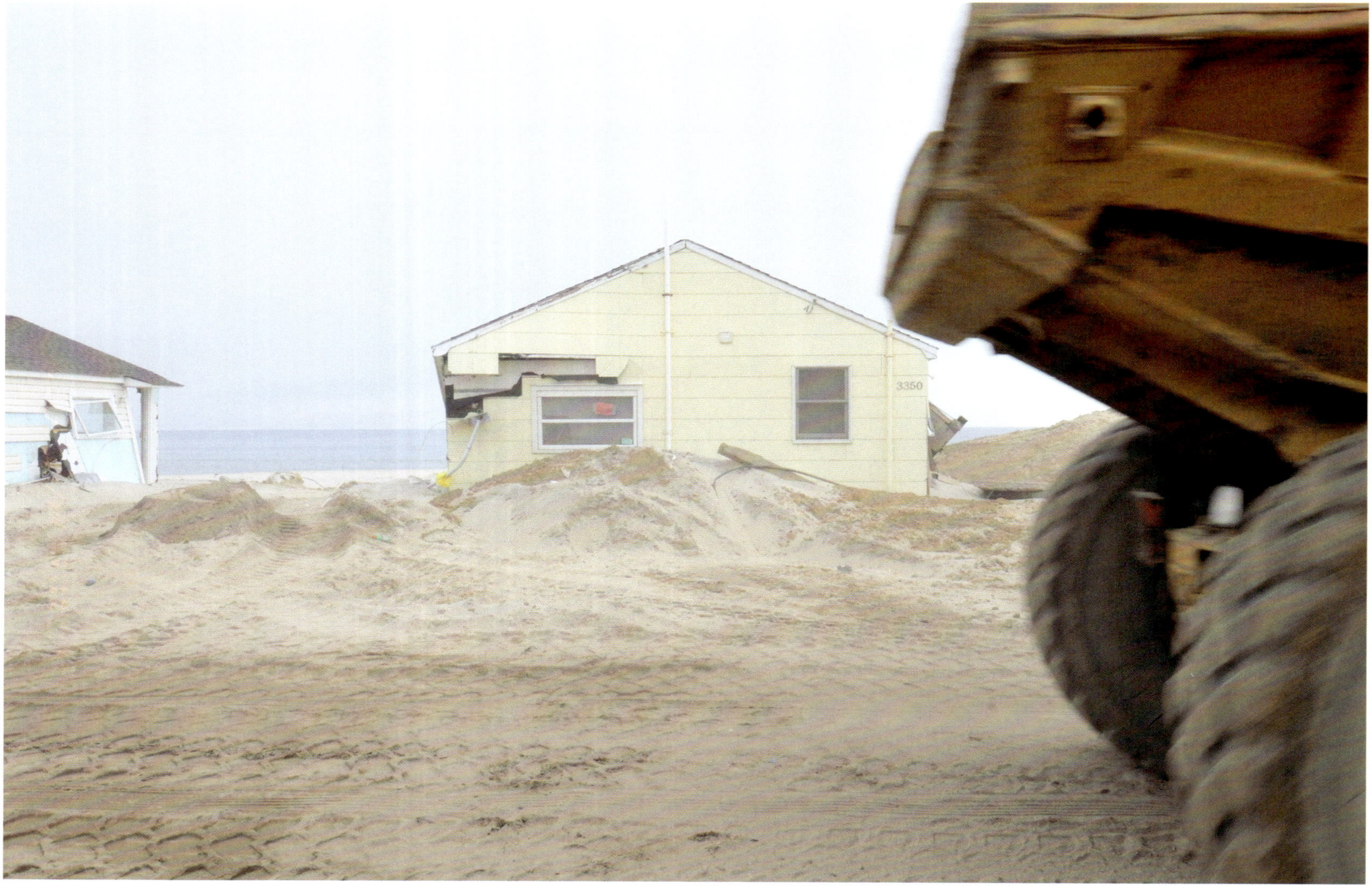
3350

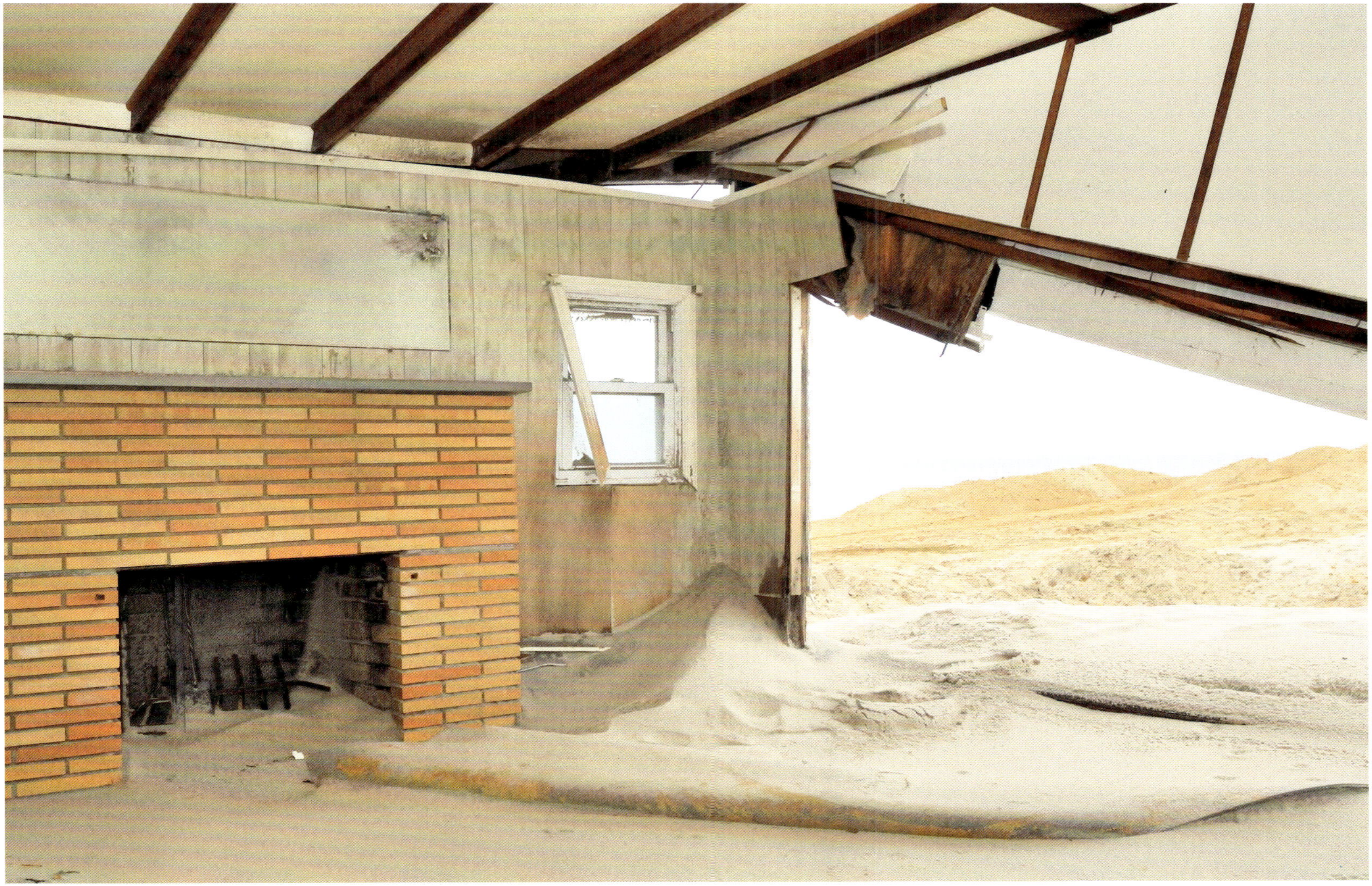

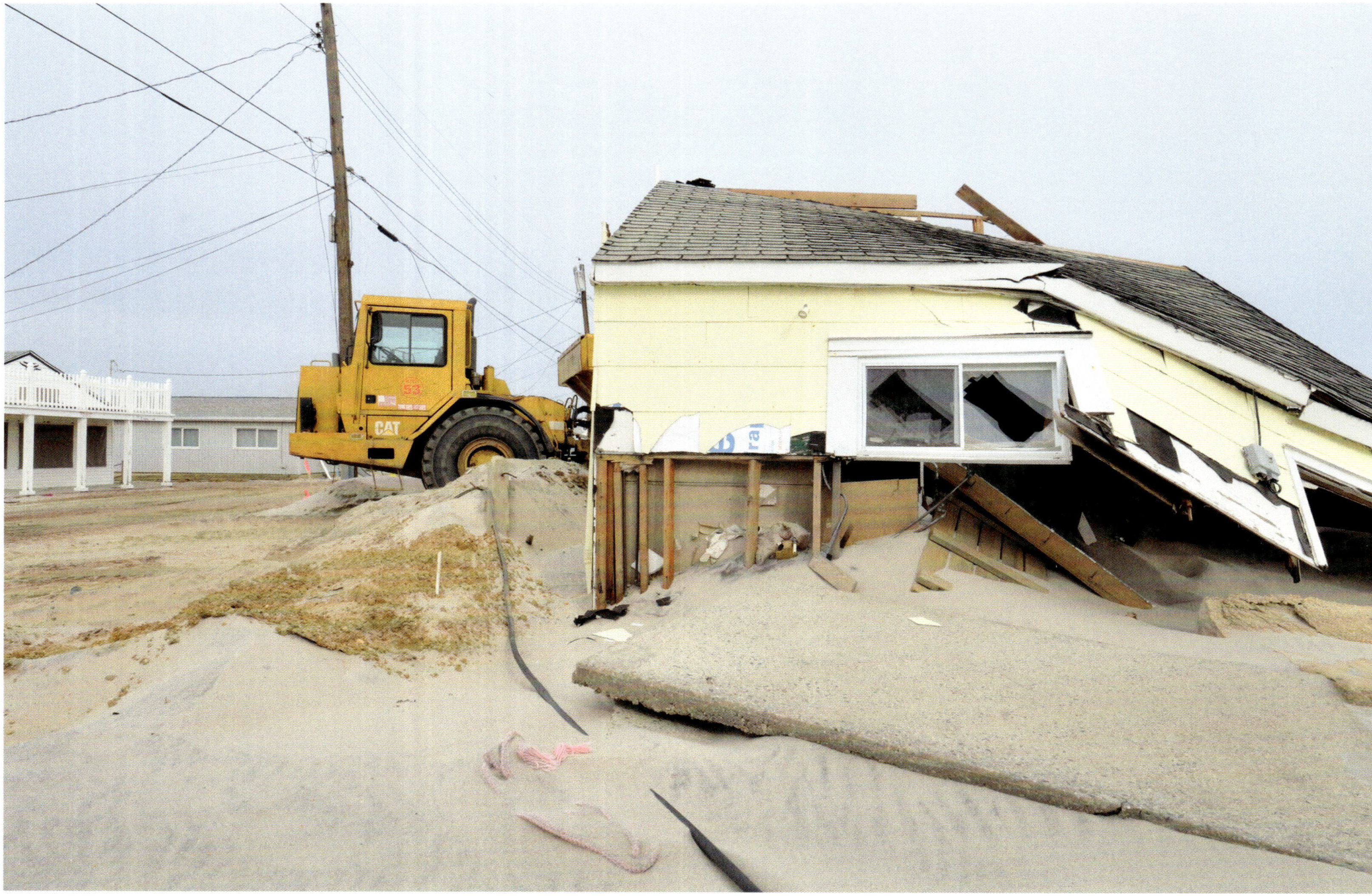
53
CAT

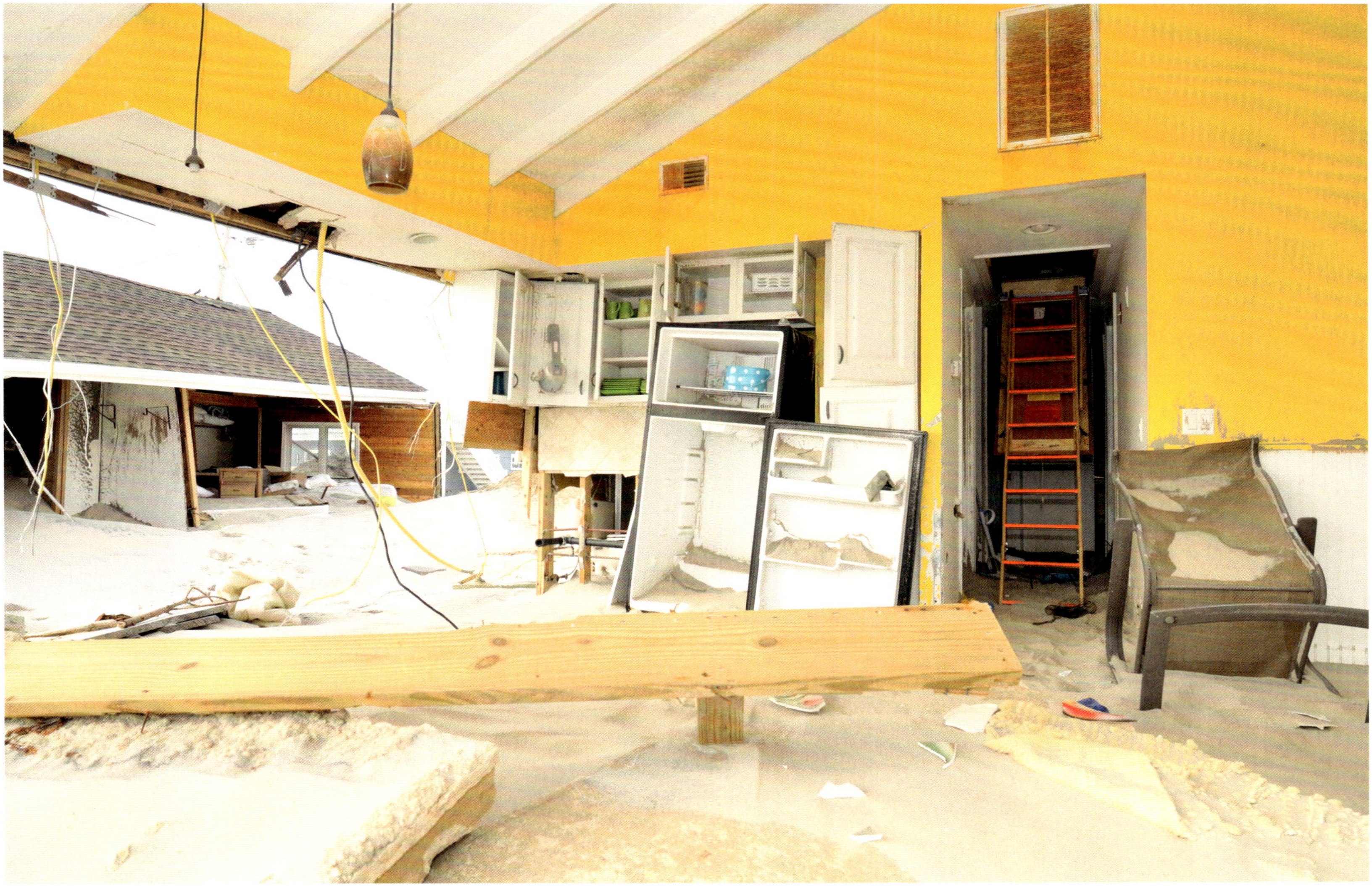

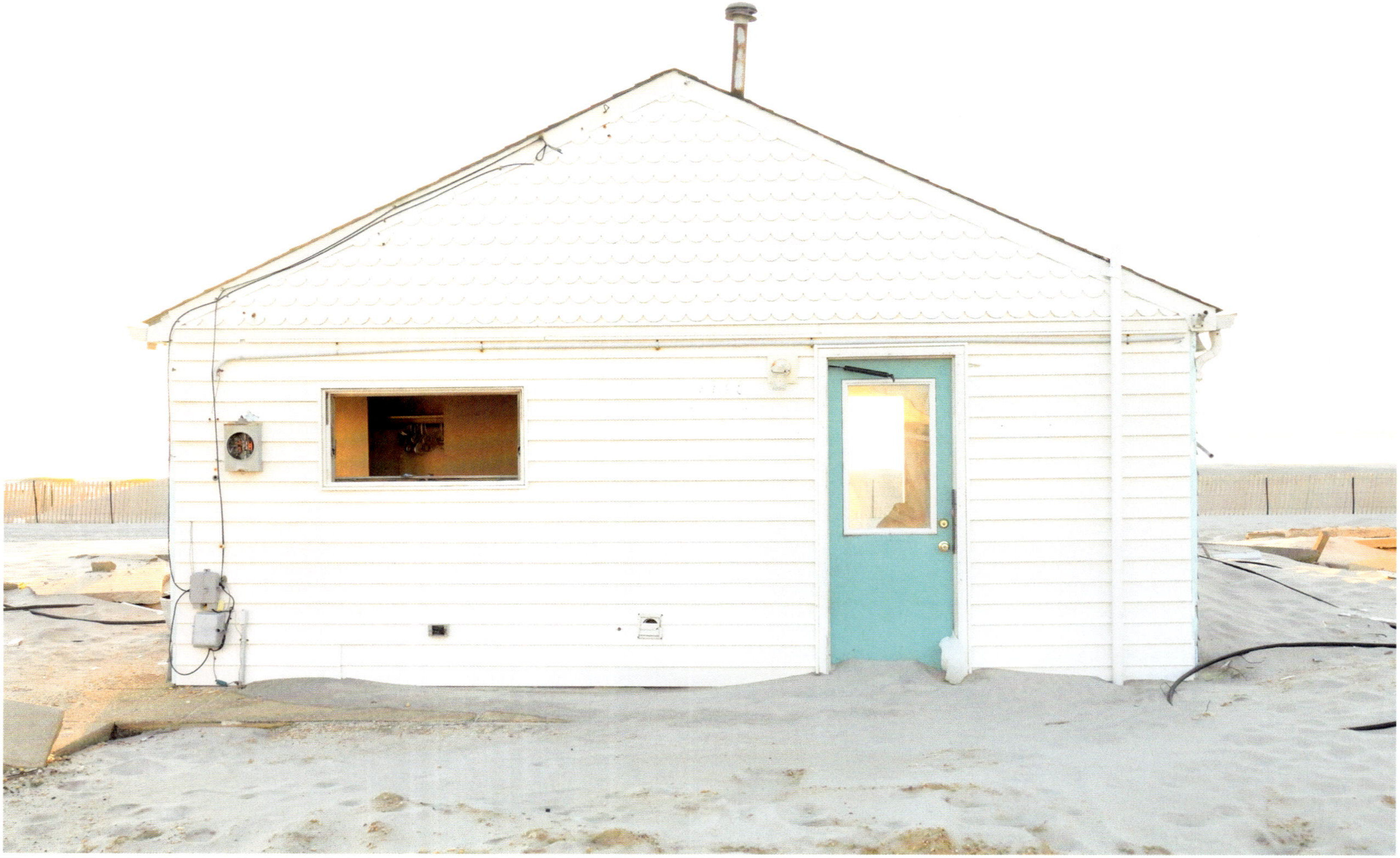

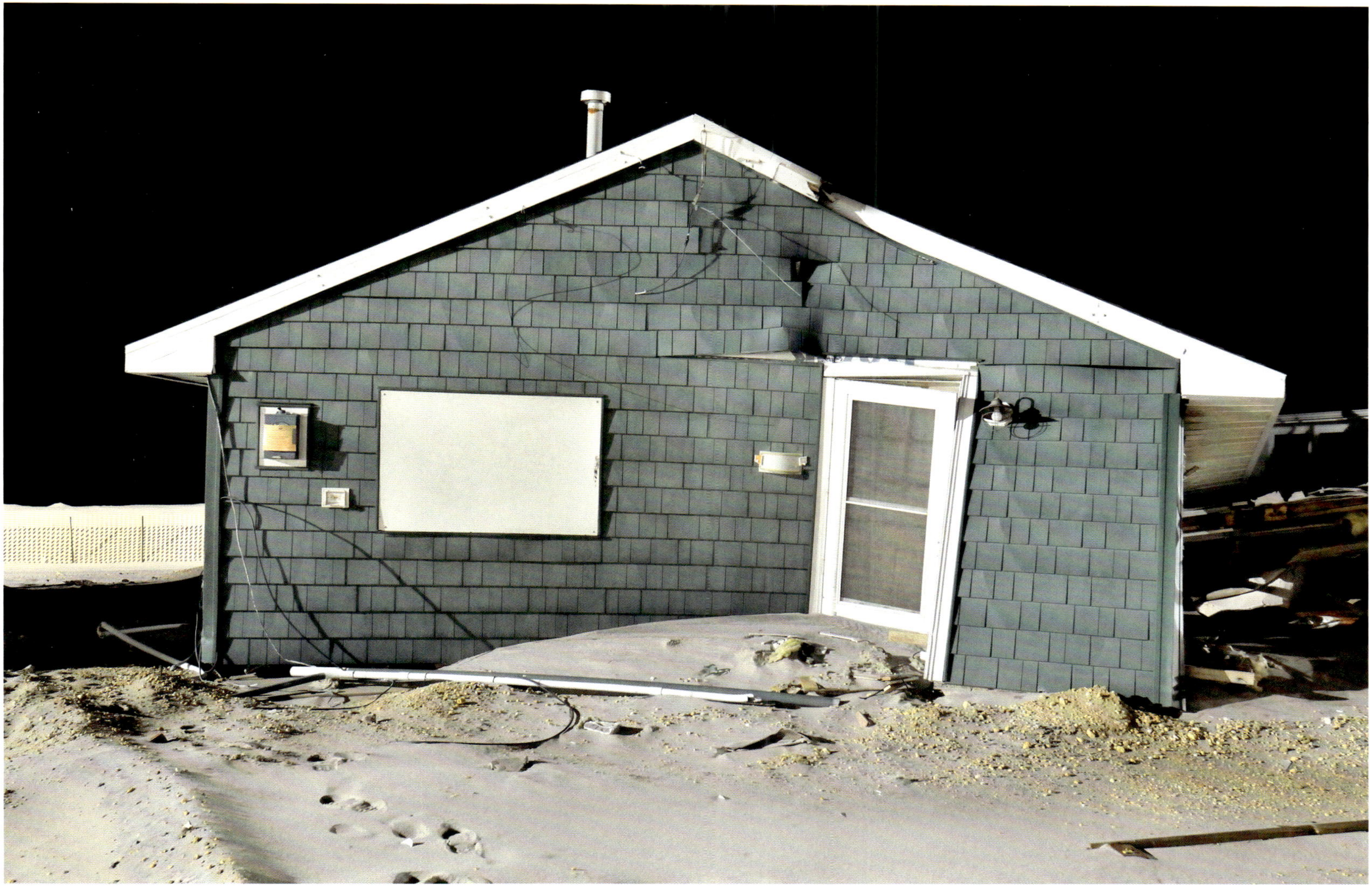

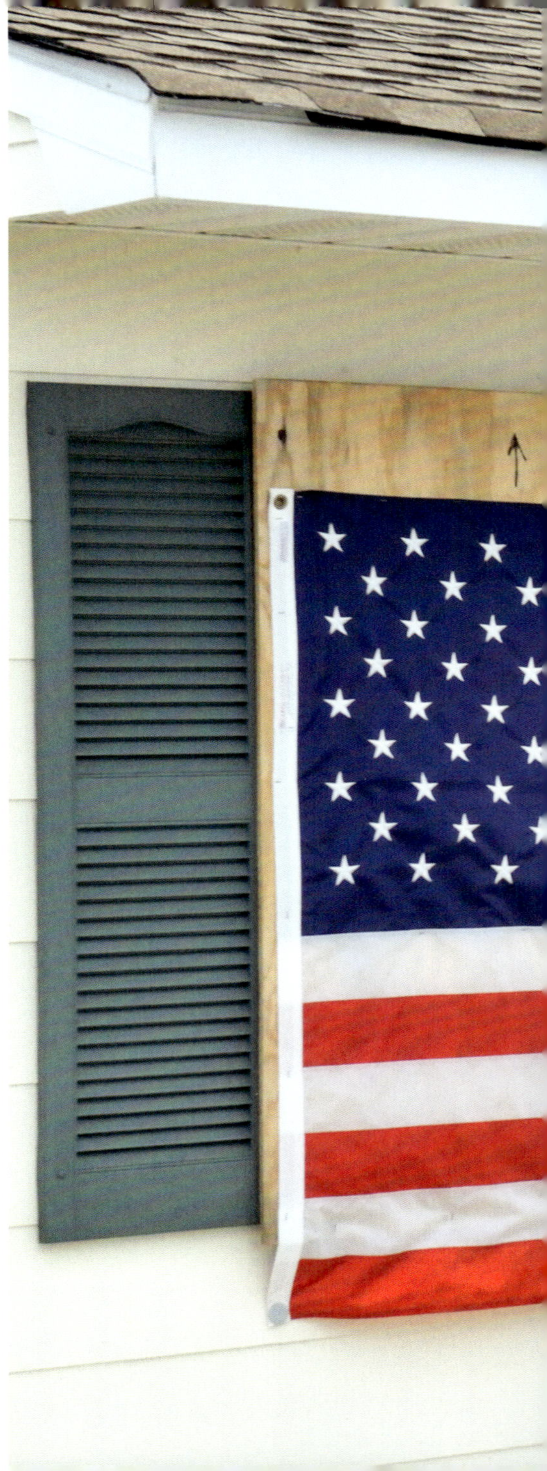

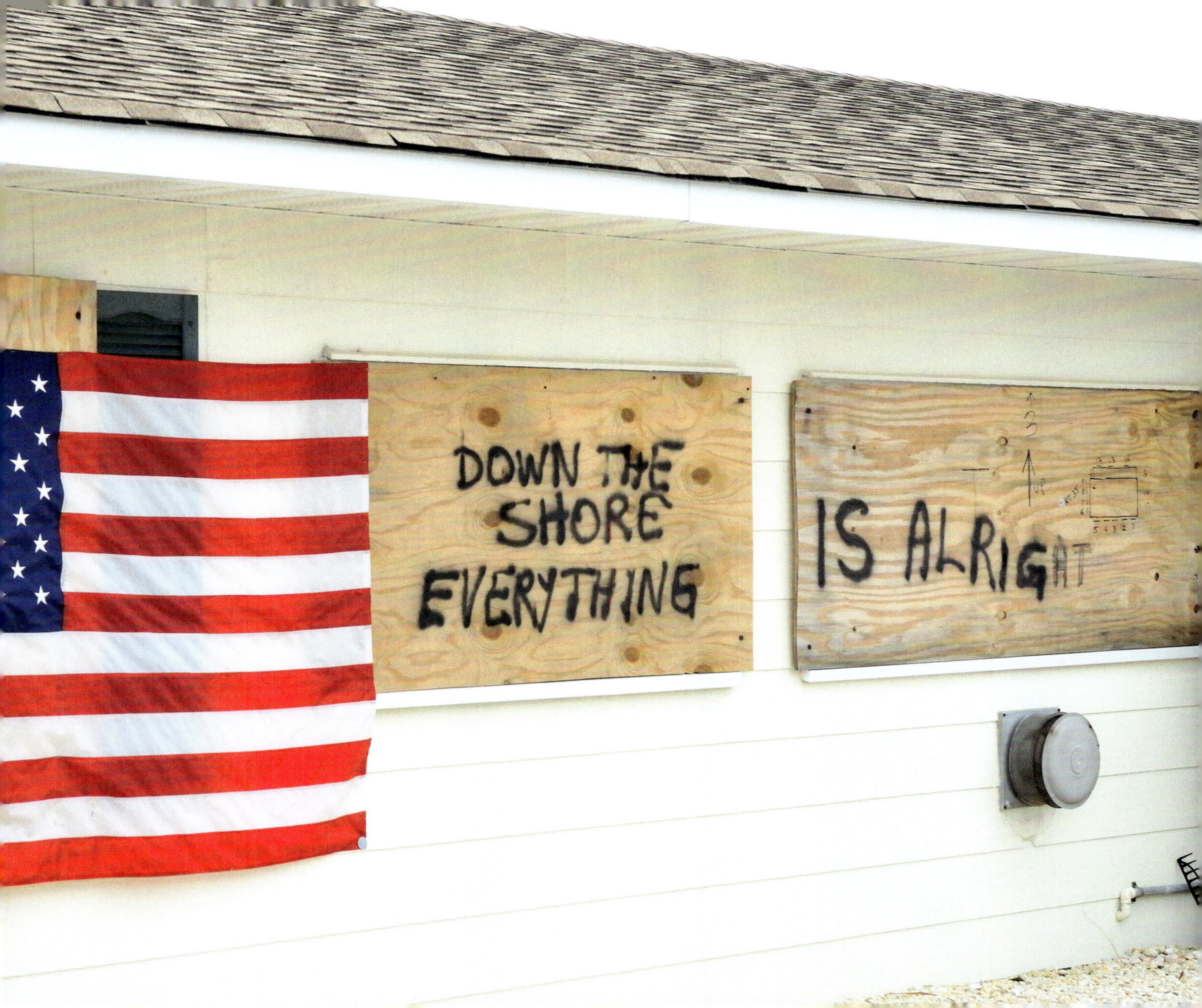
DOWN THE SHORE EVERYTHING
IS ALRIG

Texts—Harvey Benge and Steve Bisson
Copy editor—Andrew Cowin
Design—Kehrer Design Heidelberg
Image processing—Kehrer Design Heidelberg *(Patrick Horn)*
Production—Kehrer Design Heidelberg *(Tom Streicher)*

Thanks to Debra Klomp Ching, Stella Kramer, the wonderful people at the Ocean Beach Sales & Rental Agency; Brian, Jeff, Nicole, Jennifer, Scott, and owner John R. McDonough, for your continued support.

Bibliographic information published by the Deutsche Nationalbibliothek. The Deutsche Nationalbibliothek lists this publication in the Deutsche Nationalbibliografie; detailed bibliographic data are available on the Internet at *http://dnb.d-nb.de*.

Printed and bound in Germany

ISBN 978-3-86828-403-4

Kehrer Heidelberg Berlin
www.kehrerverlag.com